Praise for *Bits of*

C000079384

'Leith is never more fascinating t
things he's supposed to be writing :
parentheses, his random insights
(and considerable) talents lie . . .
accessible, true-life version of , .
brilliant' *Daily Mail*

'He's an extremely good writer. Very funny . . . wonderfully forensic . . .
His analysis of why our monetary system is the root of all evil is bordering
on genius, such is its simplicity and confidence . . . And his super-macro-
explanation of humanity's impending ruin is wonderful' *Sunday Times*

'A frontline dispatch from Leith's middle age . . . very funny. He writes in
a sort of whimsical stream of consciousness . . . even his most random
disquisitions contain glorious nuggets of information . . . Leith inter-
weaves his personal deconstruction with a broader analysis of why
everything around us seems to be getting worse' *Observer*

'Resembles an expertly-paced stand-up routine . . . He's very good at riffs
that feel, at the outset, recklessly faltering and digressive, but scramble
back on track just in time, and his use of the Omaha Beach massacre as a
metaphor for his beleaguered immune system is positively Izzard-esque'
Time Out

'Hilarious and touching and beautifully written . . . Philip Larkin meets
Jeremy Clarkson, but in a good way. This is a middle-aged *The Catcher in
the Rye*' Jon Ronson

'A skilfully crafted, controlled narrative about losing control . . . an
entertaining, esoteric, thought-provoking experience . . . Leith's ways
of thinking and writing are full of vitality and wit . . . A refreshing take
on the perils of middle age' *Irish Examiner*

'Intelligent, articulate and educated' *Sunday Telegraph*

'Fine, blackly comic writing and frequent tangents that end up in
memorable tracts of personal history . . . You never know where Leith
is going next' *Metro*

'A fascinating, shambling, often very funny meditation on failure,
remorse, physical frailty, the fear of death and the fear of pretty much
everything else . . . There's a very original mind working here' *Spectator*

BITS OF ME ARE FALLING APART

Dark Thoughts from the Middle Years

WILLIAM LEITH

BLOOMSBURY
LONDON · BERLIN · NEW YORK

First published in Great Britain 2008

This paperback edition published 2009

Copyright © 2008 by William Leith

The moral right of the author has been asserted

No part of this book may be used or reproduced in any manner
whatsoever without written permission from the Publisher except in the
case of brief quotations embodied in critical articles or reviews

Bloomsbury Publishing Plc
36 Soho Square
London W1D 3QY

www.bloomsbury.com

Bloomsbury Publishing, London, New York and Berlin

A CIP catalogue record for this book
is available from the British Library

ISBN 978 0 7475 9669 1

10 9 8 7 6 5 4 3 2 1

Typeset by Hewer Text UK Ltd, Edinburgh
Printed and bound by CPI Group (UK) Ltd, Croydon, CR0 4YY

The paper this book is printed on is certified independently in accordance with the
rules of the FSC. It is ancient-forest friendly. The printer holds chain of custody

MIX
Paper from
responsible sources
FSC
www.fsc.org   FSC® C013604

To my son, Billy

Chapter 1

I wake up, middle-aged and cranky, on an old mattress. Half of my life has gone. I piece the facts together. I'm on an old mattress because I'm sleeping in my office. I'm sleeping in my office because I always sleep in my office. I always sleep in my office because my office is my home. My office is my home because my relationship has broken up.

My relationship has broken up because . . .

Because.

I look at the sky. It is a terrifying pale sky with streaky clouds. I must have fallen asleep without closing the curtains. Looking around me, my gaze is followed, and sometimes overtaken, by a shoal of vitreous floaters, shadows cast on my retina by broken-off bits of my inner eye. Bits of me are falling apart. Bits of me are starting to return to a previous life, of being even smaller bits, and those bits, in turn, are preparing to break into smaller bits yet.

It's a Billy day – a day I will see my son – which makes me both joyful and terrified, the joy of seeing my son tempered by my fear of what will happen when I see his mother. When I see her, the quality of my thinking, always variable, can collapse into a form of dementia I had, until recently, never known. And I just can't seem to think my way out of the problem. Other middle-aged guys tell me they have similar trouble with their golf swings. Something familiar, like the ability to hit a small, dense ball, or to talk with authority, or even coherence, to the mother of your son, just goes, just . . . *goes*, and if you try to think about it, you can make things a lot worse before they get better.

And now I remember it's the last time I'll see my son for two weeks, because he's going on holiday; he's going on holiday with his mother. But I'm not going.

I was supposed to go, but things didn't work out.

So today I will be saying goodbye.

I pull myself into a sitting position, something I've got a lot better at since I started doing Pilates several months ago. Now I can sit up almost perfectly, because I have regular sessions with a coach whose job it is to teach me to sit up. I spend maybe two full hours a week practising sitting up. I can sit up better than I've been able to since I was a kid, when everything came naturally. Now that my body is failing, some things do not come naturally. They come unnaturally, which is a lot better than nothing.

I'm doing everything I can to halt the ageing process. No overeating. Regular herbal tea. Lots of water. A particular kind of porridge in the morning. Very little bread, but a lot of fruit. A great deal of brisk walking. I walk an average of 15,000 steps per day. And, although a lot of research seems to show that a single glass of red wine in the evening would be beneficial, I'm teetotal.

Maybe I'll give drinking one more chance. But not soon.

Also, I quit smoking and I don't take drugs. I used to do these things when I was younger, when my brain and body needed them less; now that my withering and corrupted tissues cry out for these stimulants, I can't have them.

There's a book next to my bed – *Power Aging* by Gary Null. I borrowed it from my father. He's eighty, and there's not much he can do. But me – I *can* do something. Sure, I'm ageing. But what sort of ageing am I doing?

Power ageing.

Science tells me that if I avoid bad things, and do good things – and if I'm not one of the 10 or so per cent who get hit by something nasty in middle age – I can be healthy, in a physical sense, for quite a while.

Psychologically I'm not so sure.

If you want to know the truth, I'm not feeling good right now. I'm tired and depleted, declining and falling, listless, indecisive. I feel like a footballer in his sad final season – playing through pain. I feel like the Dennis Quaid character in *Any Given Sunday*, one of Oliver Stone's several movies about male inadequacy. Quaid is the ageing quarterback – injured, slow, worried about the younger guy who might take his place, more worried still about the unknowable void that is just beginning to come into view. The first time you see it, the first time you see the void, it looks *really* close, like a full moon on a warm summer night; you just turn a corner and there it is. You can almost touch it.

I let go of my sitting position and then – boof! – I'm back down on the mattress, looking up at the stippled paint on the ceiling, which depresses me.

I'm forty-seven. I didn't want to say that. I wanted to wait a while before I said that. In fact, I have an urge to say something else: I don't *feel* forty-seven. But this is not strictly true, is it?

I feel forty-seven physically, and I feel forty-seven mentally.

What else is there?

Anyway, four years ago, when I was single, I felt like a superannuated teenager, and now I feel like a divorced, middle-aged dad living in an office. It's all happened so fast. You spend the

3

first half of your life learning how to make things move quickly, and you succeed, and then you wake up in the middle of your life and you feel like Rip Van Winkle.

In the Pink Floyd song 'Time', Roger Waters – I think it's him – sings about letting your life slip, as if you've missed the starting gun. When I first heard those lines, at the age of sixteen, I thought: 'I'll never make *that* mistake. I'll never miss the starting gun. I'll hear it loud and clear. Bang! How sad and pathetic, to miss the starting gun.'

Whenever I think of this, I remember a teenage English lesson. We were studying a poem by Philip Larkin about a sad old man – autobiographical, I suppose, in that Larkin always seemed to be a sad old man, even when he was quite young. The teacher asked us to sum up our feelings about the man in the poem, and one boy wrote that the man was 'hanging on in quiet desperation', quoting the Floyd song. And the teacher said, 'What a brilliant line – you've captured it exactly!' And we all laughed inwardly, thinking we'd somehow hoodwinked him, because everybody knew that Pink Floyd was the opposite of Philip Larkin – Floyd being for young people and Larkin being for sad old people.

Later, in that same lesson, we looked at another Larkin poem about a man who throws an apple core at a wastepaper basket, and misses, and then realises that he was always destined to miss, even before he started eating the apple.

I thought, 'I'll never feel like that.'

Now, if anybody put me on the spot, I'd say it was my favourite poem.

So when I say I feel forty-seven physically, and also mentally, but in some other, elusive way I *don't* feel forty-seven I suppose I mean that I've only just started feeling anything like my age; nearly all my memories seem to be those of a young man. I've only just crossed the border. Until very, very recently I did not

4

feel like the man in the poem. And now, when I look at my former self, I can see that former self clearly out of the corner of my eye. But when I try to get a better perspective, the image blurs.

Occludes, I think is the word – a word I feel able to use with less embarrassment now that I have reached this great age.

I'm seeing a lot of estate agents right now, and I've become familiar with the way they look at me when I talk about needing a garden and a room for my son, who will be living with me at the weekends. I have, in fact, just made a low offer on a house that would be ideal. I'm terrified of getting caught at the top of the market, a real possibility. The market looks poised to drop right now. In fact, I'm in danger of being skewered in the worst possible way, because, while lenders react fast to a jittery market, prices take longer to fall. So I might end up paying sky-high interest on a falling asset. On the other hand, I'm terrified of missing out on the house.

That aside, what I was talking about was the look estate agents give me. It's that divorce-nod, that slight wince, meaning 'I understand your pain'. It's not a bad look. It's sympathetic.

I'm at a certain stage in life, it says.

It happens to most guys.

More than half of guys.

So I'm not alone.

If I see a film these days, or read a book, I always identify with the divorced guy. Sitting up again, on my 'sitting bones', as my Pilates teacher calls them – 'right up on the sitting bones, William!' – I think of a film, not even a very good film, with, I think, Billy Crystal and Paul Reiser as divorced guys, meeting in a car park, with a shopping mall or fast-food area in the background, and they were smiling; I think they were smiling.

For lots of guys, this – smiling through, with other divorced guys, in car parks – is what middle age *is*. This is it. This is life. It's normal to be falling apart among hatchbacks and station wagons. It's normal to be alone. People want to be alone these days. Or, rather, they want to be together, but they can't bear the compromises involved. For instance, I keep reading about the death throes of monogamy. And it's not just monogamy – it's the whole culture, the whole thing.

The death of monogamy is part of a pattern, a linked network of things happening all across our culture.

Money, work, love, education, sport, happiness – they're all getting old.

This is what I'm thinking about, as I wake up on a mattress in my office, which is my home, because my relationship has broken up.

It's not just me is what I'm thinking.

But maybe it is. Maybe it is just me.

One of the most common symptoms of middle age, psychologists tell us, is thinking that everything around you is getting old, too. As your body and brain begin to wear out, you enter an existential crisis. You become disappointed with the world. You begin to think you can see through things, as if you've got X-ray vision. You look at the politician, but you see the hands of the puppeteer. You become conspiracy-minded. You obsess about the big questions. You obsess about small things, too, because you start seeing patterns.

And the pattern is always the same. Things are falling apart, just like you. Tiny cracks are appearing in the system, in the same way that tiny cracks are appearing in the systems that govern your body and your brain.

You can see them, these tiny cracks, in the world around you. You can see them because really you're seeing yourself. That's the classic definition of a mid-life crisis.

But there is, of course, another possibility. What if it's not just me?

What if it's me *and* the world around me?

What if the tiny cracks are real?

Something tragic happens to you when you enter your forties. People stop believing that you have the capacity to change. They think they know your future, because they know your past. (Maybe they're right.) I've got a bad past – a past full of poor decisions, dreaminess, procrastination, and every imaginable type of overconsumption and profligacy. I was unhappy as a teenager, but lived well in my twenties; I didn't want my twenties to end. I wanted to stay in the limbo of my twenties, which made my thirties difficult. In my thirties, I entered a period of denial, drink- and drug-fuelled denial; I didn't want to grow up, didn't want to face reality, didn't want to settle down – and, being a man, didn't have a body clock to tell me the real time. I can't believe I just used that as an excuse. I really can't.

Over the years of denial, I became more and more indecisive. If I wanted to put a positive spin on it, I'd say that I always want to learn more about things before I make a decision. So I tend to learn a lot, without making any decisions, which means that knowledge builds up in my head and then starts to decay, like garden compost, and if I'm not careful, my mind grows weeds.

That's the positive spin.

Negative spin: I'm a lazy – what, bastard? Fucker? Fucker is probably best. *Old* fucker. I'm a lazy old fucker. In fact, currently not even a fucker. A lazy old *fuck*.

That's the negative spin.

Also, I tend to dwell on bad things. Any self-help guru will tell you that if you focus on bad things, bad things will come to you. That's the whole idea behind the recent self-help blockbuster *The Secret*. It's a very simple idea dressed up as a fancy philosophy. It's supposedly based on the fact that everything in the world is made of tiny particles held together by forces we can't understand.

Well, that's true – nobody understands the mechanism that makes tiny particles stick together, nor why they fall apart. It's a mystery. Things stick together, and then, later, they fall apart.

But the secret behind *The Secret*, as far as I can see, is this: when you think, you harness some of the mysterious energy that makes objects hold together. So when, for instance, you think about good things, good things happen to you. This, of course, sounds highly improbable.

But I know that when you think about bad things, bad things happen.

And right now, I can't help thinking about the same few things. And these things are as follows.

Death.

Disease.

Failure.

Humiliation.

Loss.

I wish I could turn a corner, and not think about these things any more.

Damn! I'm lying in bed, thinking about a popular self-help book. At my age! Mind you, I'd love to write a popular self-help book. In fact, I'd love to write anything. Mostly, I sit at my computer, and stare at the screen, and write nothing, or hardly anything. I am full of false starts. Which would have been fine twenty or even ten years ago. Now I'm too old for false starts. In any case, I haven't been happy with anything I've written for about . . . well, ever. Recently I tried, for about the tenth time, to write a story about a man who runs away from his own wedding. In this version, you keep thinking he's selfish, noncommittal, or possibly a terminal womaniser. But it turns out he's terminally *ill*. I've also been trying to write something about a man who's having an affair and then gets cancer. He's unhappily married, but does not want to leave his wife. He dithers. The woman he's having the affair with is the love of his life, and finally, at last, he decides to leave his wife . . . and he gets cancer. The cancer is terminal. And now he realises that he must either end his affair, and die with the woman he no longer loves, or leave his wife. But – and here's the thing – he wouldn't be leaving her to *live* with the other woman. He'd be leaving his wife to *die* with the other woman. The key scene is this: his new woman comes into the hospital – but as a colleague, she only gets *one visit*. Did I say she's a colleague? She is, anyway. And this one visit she can have is in front of the guy's wife. And afterwards, the wife and the girlfriend walk out of the hospital together and share a brief, intense moment, and you begin to think the wife has known all along, and it's sort of cheesy and a bit creepy. Meanwhile, the guy is failing, slipping away . . .

I'm thinking he should jump out of his bed and escape. Fight his way across town, fighting decrepitude and possibly even dementia.

Would this be good? With Harrison Ford in the lead role? If it's not good, I've got several more variations – dying politicians, football coaches and so on. And then I've got some ideas about people having mental breakdowns. All very cheesy. But still – I read this memoir the other day, *Tuesdays with Morrie*, about a dying professor. The author, a guy who hadn't paid attention in class, meets his old teacher, who is dying of a wasting disease. This author is sort of rich but overworked. The old professor tells him what's *really* important: family, honesty, learning to love the little things. The stuff you knew all along. Anyway, they meet, every Tuesday, and they eat sandwiches, and the author, his name is Mitch, notices heartbreaking details about the guy's curtains and carpets, and the old professor dies, but very, very bravely. The message, I suppose, is that death is part of life, so you'd better understand this while you've still got time to do something with your life. Good message. Sure, it's cheesy – it's major cheese. But it's good. It works. When I start to think that my stories might be a little on the cheesy side, I think about *Tuesdays with Morrie*.

In any case, it's all academic. I never get beyond the outline stage. And right now, professionally speaking, I'm thinking about something else entirely. A few weeks ago, I went to a conference organised by a glossy magazine. This whole thing was in a hotel. We sat around in teams, one team per table, and chatted about possible subjects for articles. I mentioned this thing I'd heard about on the radio several months ago, and then Googled. Things moved fast: later that day, I found myself giving a little speech, based on the radio item, in front of the magazine's staff. I put quite a lot into it, actually.

I remember saying something like: 'The quality of today's dog food is a *scandal*, and vets are doing nothing about it! After all, why should they? When dog food is bad, dogs get ill, and that means more work for the vet. So vets *want* dog food to be bad. Vets *love* dog food being bad. What dogs need is not tinned mush – it is *raw meaty bones*. Thank you.'

There was applause.

Now my writer's block (but I *hate* that term) is worse than ever.

Until recently, I couldn't write a story about a man dying of cancer. Now I can't write a story about dog food.

Something inside my mind, I'm pretty sure, is slipping, some cog or wheel or pulley, slipping, slipping, past the point of no return.

*   *   *

10

Every time I have a relationship, the bulk of it consists of me working on my bad qualities, while the other person waits for me to change. This last relationship, though, has been different. At forty-seven, it looks like I'm too old to change. The boat has sailed. The bird has flown. Isn't that what somebody said after the Gunpowder Plot? My memory, which used to be very clear, very sharp on detail, is no longer the muscular, tuned-up search engine it once was. 'The birds have flown.' That's what he said, whoever he was, somebody Pym I think, and what he meant was that the conspirators had escaped. 'Very witty,' I thought, sitting in the classroom, at my desk with its hinged lid, the wood practically black with age. I really thought 'the birds have flown' was a witty thing to say. That's because I thought people from the past were generally very po-faced about things, so saying something like 'the birds have flown' was, in the context of a history lesson, extremely witty.

I'm digressing. What happens when you reach a certain age is that, to make up for the mental faculties you've lost, you gain a tendency to digress. My point, anyway, was going to be that, when people say you're as old as you feel, they're wrong. You're not as old as *you* feel – as old, that is, as you think you are. No – you're as old as *other people* think you are.

Just like the stock market – it's only as good as people think it is. It's only as good as it appears to be.

I like to think the birds have not flown, by the way. I like to think I have not crossed the line, when it comes to the formation of my character, in the same way that I don't think I crossed the Smoking Line, or the Drinking Line. I don't want to be doomed to remain as the person I am now.

I can change!

I have faith!

But I also know that this is the sort of faith that characterises our modern world, and is ruining it. We all want to believe that we have not yet grown up. We all want to believe that change is possible, that we can re-invent ourselves forever. We think we'll find something else when the oil has gone. We're always hoping we can take out a loan we'll never have to pay back. We're beginning to believe in nothing less than our own immortality.

And that, I sometimes think, is the truly tragic thing.

I must get out of bed. As usual, I do not feel great – I do not feel *myself*. I have pinpricks of pain in my temples. Later, they will pound. They always pound from the middle of the day onwards. I feel dizzy when I stand up. Lights flash in my eyes, also when I stand up. I have pimples on my forehead, a symptom that has been linked to stomach problems. I have butterflies in my stomach. I have a partially cricked neck. There is a lump, possibly a muscle knot, possibly not a muscle knot, on the left of the base of my neck. I first noticed it two years ago, and it hasn't changed. My policy has been to do nothing, to see if I can ride it out.

I have mild toothache, and a tender jaw from grinding my teeth in the night. The right side of my throat does not hurt, but did yesterday, when I experienced a shooting, electric shock-like pain. But not to worry. This happens often. My heart feels weird. It flutters. Sometimes it seems to stop for about two seconds, and then catch up, flapping like a startled bird. There is a dull ache in my abdomen. Sometimes there is a sharper ache in my abdomen. That's the current bowel situation. My left thigh is numb all the way down the outside, from hip to knee. There is no feeling there. This part of my thigh has been without feeling for about a year. It's the way I sit at my desk, I hope.

I do have lower-back pain, but this is nothing compared to the lower-back pain I had before I started doing Pilates. I have a stiff shoulder from an injury sustained during a sliding-downstairs incident in Nova Scotia in 1979, when I was eighteen years old and visiting my father in his snowbound house-in-the-woods. Something is wrong with my left knee. But then, something has been wrong with my left knee for ever, just like something has been wrong with my left ankle for ever. In fact, my left ankle is, if anything, better than it has been for twenty years.

I do not have erectile dysfunction. All I've noticed is that, when I have sex often, it takes longer to reach orgasm. That's all I've noticed. And I sympathised with Vince Vaughn in the movie *Wedding Crashers*, during the scene in which he is tied up by the sex-mad woman with red hair, who has made him have sex over and over, and now wants it again. I could sense he had that tired, aching-cock feeling you get, after the first flush of youth, not that you've had a bad time exactly, but just that your penis needs a rest. It's been pumped up, and squeezed, and gripped, and kneaded, and sucked, and possibly bitten, and pushed into places that are relatively tight, or even very tight, and that's fine, because all this time you have been filled with painkilling hormones. And then these painkilling hormones wear off; after the age of twenty-five or so, they will not come back for an encore – not on the same day. Anyway, I sympathised with Vince Vaughn, lying on the bed there, his wrists tied to the bed posts, and I know that, until I was twenty-five or so, I would not have sympathised with him.

I've regained most of the feeling in the fingers of my right hand. Slightly more than a year ago, I broke up some concrete in the back garden of the house I was living in, or sort of living in, with the mother of my son. Her house. She knocked down a shed at the end of the garden, and underneath the shed was this thick concrete base. We hired a big, juddering drill. On the same day I bought some boots with high steel toecaps.

The drilling was fine. When I say the drilling was fine, I mean that, before long, I had worked out a good technique. You'd think the drill would work best when it vibrates the most, wouldn't you? Well, that's not true. You have to slow down the vibrations. Then you get into a sort of 'drilling zone'. It's a physics thing, and I think it can be related to the way sonic toothbrushes work.

I drilled for seven hours. At the time, the fact that I couldn't feel my fingers felt pretty normal, just about what you'd expect. A day or so later, most of the feeling came back into my left hand. But the right hand remained numb for months, the feeling gradually creeping back upwards, and now I've got everything back except for a slight tingle at the tip of my right middle finger.

There's a lump in the muscle at the front of my right shin. It's pretty big, and smooth, and hard, like the cartilage on the round end of a beef bone, or a ball bearing. Sometimes it's painful. It appeared in 1999, so I don't think it can be cancer. It announced itself as a pain, during a trip to California, when I was very overweight and drinking too much – when I was very messed up, and in denial. I was drinking and smoking and taking drugs, because I felt that doing these things would help me to stay young. It wasn't working. I was in a bad state – at the low point of a difficult relationship, in debt, and snorting lots of drugs. I kept getting nosebleeds.

I had this terrible nosebleed all over a Japanese-American woman who I was sitting next to on a plane.

But I won't get into that. This is about the leg lump.

The week of the leg lump, I went to Los Angeles to interview an actress. I was hoping the actress would tell me something racy, so that lots of magazines would want to reprint my article, thus getting me out of debt, thus giving me some breathing space to tackle my drink and drug problems, to tackle the fact that I was drinking because I couldn't face the future, drinking to feel like I did when I was in my twenties – although, of course, when I was in my twenties, I didn't drink very much at all, because I had no need to get drunk every night to prove to myself how young I was. Anyway, in 1999 I was in a bad state. I was shitting blood, if you want to know the truth.

When I did the interview I was desperately hung-over. We were sitting in a trailer, which sounds glamorous but wasn't – it was a caravan on a sloping gravel track on the edge of a field. In the trailer I settled down and fiddled with my tape recorders. When I interview someone, I always try to give the impression of being simultaneously confused and anxious, which puts people at their ease. I then tell the person that my first question is a hard one, but that I've decided to bite the bullet and ask the hardest question first.

Then I say, 'If you could tell me the story of your life so far, in one breath, what would you say?'

And often the person, who was expecting a question about sex or drugs, relaxes. On this occasion, the actress began to talk about troubling events in her childhood, and then said, 'Once I hit twelve, late eleven or twelve, some other events took place which informed my person a great deal more.'

There it was – a possible story, a revelation of pain, of how childhood pain stays with you, the sort of sad story that people like to read. I felt myself drowning in mixed feelings. On the one hand, I could pursue this thing, ferret it out; I might sell the story to many magazines, might get out of debt. On the other hand . . . was this what my life had come to? I was thirty-nine. I had a drink problem. I was shitting blood. I had dull aches and sharp, needling pains in every part of my abdomen. I spent my mornings in a sludgy haze and my afternoons in a mounting storm of panic and paranoia. One Sunday afternoon, not long before this, I had got out of bed after a terrific bender, leaving my girlfriend in bed, gone for a long walk, and become possessed with the feeling that I must have murdered her in the night, without any

15

evidence to support this feeling; but it had grown, had escalated to the point of near-certainty, and I'd phoned and she hadn't picked up, and I'd phoned again, and again, sweating in the street, and when she finally came to the phone, and said, 'What is it? What do you keep calling for?' I jabbered something meaningless and she hung up, and I carried on walking, probably more disturbed than I had been before I'd called. And here I was, pushing forty, sitting in a trailer on a sloping gravel track on the edge of a field, prying into the pain of an actress, hoping to find a route to more pain, pain that would be valuable to me. I sat there in the trailer, wanting a drink, and went back to Los Angeles afterwards and got drunk in the bar of the Four Seasons Hotel. The next day, a bright, sharp winter day, I woke up in another sludgy haze and went for a long walk. I walked all day – four hours in the morning, and then four hours in the afternoon. Towards the end of this, there was a pulling or ripping sensation in my right leg. I hobbled back to my hotel. Then I got drunk. The next morning I felt the lump. That was eight years ago. Now I'm sober, not shitting blood, but the lump is still there, exactly the same as it was. It just appeared, and has got neither bigger nor smaller. Sometimes, particularly if I jog, the area around it frays, causing sharp pain, followed by swelling for a few days.

The story about the actress did not get me out of debt.

Might the lump be cancer? Almost certainly not, is my feeling. I'm pretty sure it's scar tissue from a muscle tear. It just *resembles* a tumour. If it was a tumour, I would be feeling seriously ill by now.

There's just one problem with this line of reasoning. I *am* feeling seriously ill. I feel dizzy and nauseous and hollow at the core, a sensation that, lately, never quite leaves me. This morning I can place this physical sensation exactly. It's how I felt on the morning of my grandfather's funeral, in May 1984. I was anxious, and I hadn't slept properly, and my bowels felt simultaneously full and locked up, and I was drained of energy but also wired, and I had a sense of dread that seemed to come from within my tissues, the exact feeling that presages a fever. The night before, I'd seen his body.

I often replay the scene. I arrive at my grandparents' house. I sit down. My grandmother pours me a cup of tea. My mother, whose father has just died, looks at me across the table, and says, 'He's here, you know.'

I can't meet her eye. Has she lost her mind?

So I say something like, 'Yes, well, of course he's here. He's probably, you know, looking down on us, right now.'

'No, that's not what I meant,' says my mother. 'I meant that he is here, in this house, right now.'

Yes, I think, she has lost her mind.

'He's in the front room,' she says. 'Go and look, if you want.'

People are nodding. I drink my tea. I get up and leave the room, and walk down the corridor, and push open the door to the front room, not absolutely sure what I will find, and then there's the painful understanding that this uncertainty is a form of denial, and of course I know what I will find, and what I find is a coffin, the top part covering only some of the bottom part, and inside the bottom part is, of course, my grandfather's body, with what looks like a handkerchief over his face, a silk cloth sort of thing, and I move backwards, back towards the door. But I can't leave the room without taking the handkerchief off his face. This would feel like a betrayal. So I walk back to the coffin. I touch the corner of the handkerchief, and lift it, and there, in the dim lamplight of the room, is my grandfather's face.

And now I can't breathe properly. The face is not exactly his face, but what appears to be a much younger version of his face, not the seventy-seven-year-old broken-veined drinker-and-

17

smoker face I knew, but a face that is at once thinner and smoother, a very pale face, just like the one from old posed photographs taken in the 1920s.

And I put the handkerchief back, and go into the other room, and find myself unable to look at anybody, filled as I am with a terrible fear that somebody else will go into the front room and look at this dead face.

I say things like, 'So, has everybody seen the coffin that wants to?'

And: 'So, have you maybe changed your mind about seeing the coffin?'

I can't say 'body'.

I can't say 'face'.

That night, I become obsessed with the idea that my brother has planned to visit the coffin while I am asleep. The thought that he will look at the face is unbearable to me. We sit up, drinking shots of whisky. Later, we go to bed, in the same bed. He passes out. I lie awake, and then fall into a troubled sleep.

In the middle of the night, he gets out of bed.

'What are you doing?'

'I'm going to the toilet.'

'Are you?'

'What?'

'Are you going to the toilet?'

'What?'

I hear the flush, and then the footsteps as he walks downstairs. I sit on the stairs and watch as he enters the kitchen, absolutely sure he knows I am watching, also absolutely sure that he plans to look at the face.

He does not.

The next day it is bright, with clouds in the sky. I have butterflies in my stomach. I am tired to the point of dizziness, but edgy. I feel weak, constipated, headachy, full of dread. I want to the day to end. But I don't want the day to end. The sight of mundane things, like plugs, and appliances, and gloss paint on a door, fills me with a sharp sense of loss.

And that's exactly how I feel now. I feel like I've been taken, via a wormhole in the space-time of my memory, to this exact place.

I wish I was somewhere else.

Now I see that I fell asleep reading *Intimate Terrorism* by Michael Vincent Miller, a book about the death of love, one of the best books I've read recently about the death of love. But I don't want to think about the death of love at this exact moment – or, rather, I want to think about it too much, and I know that, once I start, I won't be able to stop, and my mood will plummet. I can already feel it starting, the need to think about the death of love, which will lead to thinking about the death of my relationship, or rather, at best, its probable death. Maybe it's not dead but gasping, a fish out of water, and I try not to think about fish out of water, the fish you see in markets, laid out on slabs, their gills gently flapping, or stuffed into plastic bags on the beach by anglers, like the mackerel I saw last summer when I was on the beach with my son and his mother, having of course a serious discussion about things; and as we talked, the angler, who was about ten yards away, cast his line into the sea again and again, once bringing up a single mackerel, which he unhooked and stuffed into a plastic bag, and he put the bag a few feet away from where we were, before walking back down to the surf line, and the fish in the bag flapped metronomically, rustling the bag, a very disturbing sound, and I kept wanting to get up and kill the fish, or maybe take it out of the bag and throw it back in the sea.

19

The flapping stopped, and then started up again, in bursts. The bursts got shorter and shorter. I kept wondering which would be the last burst. The fish took about twenty minutes to die.

I hate lying on this mattress. But I hate the idea of doing anything else much, *much* more. Sometimes, when I feel like this, I have a personal 'bright side' conference, in which I list the good things about my life, but right now I don't quite have the mental strength for this. And, lately, a few of the good things – 'there's still time', and 'next time will be better', and 'you can learn from this' – are beginning to look old and jaded themselves. What if there isn't still time? What if there isn't a next time? What if the mole below my collar bone, which shows at least three clear signs of being cancerous, *is* cancerous? One: it's patchy. Two: the borders are uneven. Three: it's bigger than a pencil eraser. Four: it's growing. Or rather: it might be growing. Sometimes I look at it, and it looks huge, and sometimes it looks just the same as it ever was, depending on my mood.

But I can't go to see the doctor about this mole, because I have applied for life insurance, and I have given the insurance company permission to ask my doctor for my medical records, and if I were to consult my doctor before he received the insurance company's letter, and if he thought my mole was worth checking out, he would include this information in his report, and my insurance would be delayed, and my premiums would be huge, and all of this might affect my chances of getting a mortgage, and I need a mortgage, because I can't afford to buy a house outright, and I can't afford a house because houses have tripled in value in the last ten years, because of rampant inflation, which is actually the result of a scam. The house-price scam is precisely like a Ponzi scheme, which is more or less the same thing as a pyramid scheme, or a chain letter, which is pretty much the same thing as every government's mantra for success – economic growth.

And these things are worth checking out.

Trying to grasp the concept of Ponzi schemes, things that grow bigger until they can't go on any longer, I consider the lifespan of the cod. The adult cod gets bigger and bigger, until it dies. At first, growth is an advantage, because being bigger makes the cod harder to eat. So for a while growth is self-sustaining, because all the precious time the larger cod saves by not having to run away from predators can be spent looking for food. But there's a downside, which is that the ageing cod must eat more and more food to sustain its growing mass. And one day, it can't find enough food. One day, it's thriving, and the next it's just a tiny bit too big for its own good.

After that – downhill.

I think this is right, but the compost in my mind has grown weeds, and my search engine no longer resembles a line of crew-cut cops combing every inch of territory, as in the movie *Mississippi Burning*, cops searching for the bodies of the three civil rights activists, searching with 'a fine-tooth comb', which is not the same thing as a 'fine toothcomb', not the same thing at all. I've often heard people use the expression 'searching with a toothcomb', as if there were such a thing as a toothcomb, an implement you might use to comb your teeth. And this annoys me, this makes me grumpy, people talking about toothcombs, in a way that definitely did not happen when I was younger. I used to think it was funny when someone said 'toothcomb'. Now, when somebody says the word, I have an attack of rattiness; I think, 'Toothcomb! Jesus! That's exactly what's wrong with the world!'

Does the cod get bigger and bigger until it dies? I *think* so. But the search engine in my mind is not like a line of crew-cut cops combing a marsh. It's like Inspector Clouseau.

It's like Inspector Clouseau when he bumps into a man with a white stick, crashes right into him, and says, 'What is the matter with you? Are you blind?'

Did I mention that I might be starting a fever? At forty-seven, I pick up infections much more regularly than I did even a few years ago. I know this is partly because I'm exposed to infections from my son. But I have to face a bigger worry – my immune system is almost certainly getting weaker. Until I was about forty, I was one of those people who is 'never' ill. I can clearly remember, at the age of forty, boasting that I had never been ill enough to take a day off work. (This thought terrifies me. That was only seven years ago! What will the next seven bring?) It's true, though – I never took a day off work, through illness, until I was over forty. If I had a fever it usually only lasted a day and the symptoms were very mild; they started to disappear the moment I noticed them.

This makes me think of Steven Spielberg's *Saving Private Ryan*. Lying here, feeling dizzy and rough, it occurs to me that, until I was forty, I dealt with viruses in the way that the Germans dealt with those first boats on Omaha Beach on the early morning of 6 June 1944. In the movie you see the landing craft bouncing through the water. The soldiers in the craft are shaking with fear, and praying, and vomiting. One guy vomits in a way that tells you exactly how terrified he is. He squirts it out, in two jerky spasms. That's how viruses used to feel when they tried to attack me.

The next thing you see in the film is the front part of a landing craft opening, to let the soldiers get out. But they don't get out. The German guns cut them down before they can even take *one step*. That was my immune system. I was the Germans. My young immune system had, as the leading gerontologist Tom Kirkwood puts it, 'a repertoire of weapons of quite extraordinary versatility'. The first line of my defence, my white blood cells, had the ability to recognise a threat, and almost immediately mutate into appropriate defences to combat that threat.

You see a landing craft; you feed a belt of bullets into your MG-34 machine gun. You swing the gun on the tripod. You know to wait until the perfect moment. That was my immune system. I was the Germans.

Hein Severloh, the German soldier believed to have killed the most GIs on D-Day, has talked of killing every single soldier in one landing craft – that's around thirty soldiers. The front part dropped down, and he pumped hundreds of bullets into the craft in a matter of seconds. He says he can remember one man screaming into a radio. Five or ten seconds later, everybody was lying still on the floor. Severloh says he developed killing techniques, learning fast over the course of the morning of 6 June. Soldiers began to jump over the sides of their craft, to avoid being massacred before they got out. Severloh would wait until they were standing up in the water, sometimes neck-deep. Their movement through the water was painfully slow. He raked the surf with bullets and watched the men tip over. He switched between the MG-34, which he used to destroy groups of men, and a high-powered rifle, which he used to pick men off singly if they managed to separate and move up the beach. He says he can remember aiming at one man's chest, but misfiring slightly and hitting him through the centre of the forehead. The exiting bullet pulled the man's helmet off the back of his head.

Severloh killed hundreds of men, and possibly more than a thousand, in a couple of hours.

Spielberg captures it perfectly when he switches his camera from the beach, where the soldiers are dying, to the bluff, where the Germans are doing the killing. I don't think any director has managed to convey relentless killing as well as this. But it can't last for ever. When thousands of men run towards thirty machine-gun emplacements, there will eventually be attrition. One or two gunners will lose concentration; somebody picking up a belt of ammunition will trip and lose vital seconds; one man will make one bad weapon choice, using the rifle when he should have used the machine gun, or vice versa, and the mistake will let a few men through, and these men will kill one of the thirty machine gunners, and it will be a minute or two before the gunner is replaced, and the replacement gunner will take a while before he gets his eye in properly, giving the attackers a new opportunity.

This is what happens to your immune system as you enter middle age. 'The tightly regulated network of cell-to-cell inter-actions begins to get a tiny bit sloppier,' as Kirkwood puts it. Mistakes beget mistakes. Tom Hanks and his little gang of men knock out a machine-gun post, and for a few seconds they have 'defilade' – an undefended channel they can run into.

Now, when I get a fever, it lasts a few days, further weakening my defences and making my organs work harder until I ride it out. In the last year, I've been ill five or six times. The viral attacks are more frequent, and also more intense. These days, a fever means several days out of action, in a way that a fever at the age of twenty, or even thirty-nine, definitely did not. In those days, a fever was a fever, and nothing else. Now, a fever is often more than just a fever – it might easily be part of a package involving serious head and stomach pain. Earlier this year, I was felled by a fever combined with a migraine, and something else that affected my bowels; they felt like they were going to explode.

Now, at last, I understand the central truth about life.

I'm the Germans.

And you know what happened to the Germans, don't you? Everybody, in the end, is the Germans.

I'm the Germans, and Tom Hanks has arrived.

He's hiding behind a concrete bunker.

He's waiting.

Tom Hanks. I love Tom Hanks in *Saving Private Ryan* as Captain Miller; it's the fact that I'm not like Captain Miller that has often proved my downfall, Miller who is always pressed for time, but acts immediately and decisively, his brain computing what would be the best thing to do in the circumstances, and then doing it. The Alpha Male. John Wayne, Gary Cooper, Errol Flynn. Cary Grant and James Stewart were the first of a new type – strong, yes, but against a background of self-doubt. James Dean – who knows what would have happened with him? Then came Jack Lemmon, Dustin Hoffman, Woody Allen, Kevin Spacey, Bill Murray: the anti-heroes. Would Bill Murray lie on a mattress and allow himself to be overtaken by a mid-life crisis? Yes he would. He would creep out of bed late in the day, and go and have a drink and a smoke at the bar, two things I have stopped doing.

I can't even drink or smoke any more!

There are moments when I look at Tom Hanks in *Saving Private Ryan*, and I can feel the tears welling up. He's like the old guys. He runs towards the bullets, because this is better than staying still and waiting to die. He knows he will die, and probably pretty soon. At one point, he shouts, 'All we can do is die!' And when, at the very end, Ryan, now an old man, collapses, half a century later, in front of Miller's grave, we feel like collapsing too, because of the date on the neat white cross. It is: 13 June 1944. In the movie, Miller was the guy who breached the defences at Omaha Beach, the guy who won the war, you might almost say. If there were two guys who won the war, it would be him and Churchill. And yet, when he landed on the beach, he only had a week to live.

My brain is now focused on Tom Hanks as Captain Miller. I love him. I wish I could be just a bit more like him.

Thinking this, I sit up and push myself up on my feet, and stand, my head momentarily dizzy. A small firework show flickers across the screen of my retina. And then I'm all action: I grab my radio, walk shakily towards the door, open the door, put the radio on the floor of the hallway, enter the bathroom, switch on the bathroom light, place my hands on the washbasin, and lean on it, propping myself up, the extractor fan a grainy rasp in my ear.

Next, I piss, halting the flow mid-stream to check that my prostate gland is still working – it is, although this is not a comprehensive test – and then I wash my hands. I imagine my prostate as something on the outside of my urethra, like a hand gripping a hose. As you get older, the hand gets plumper, and so grips the hose more tightly, which makes it harder to force liquid through the hose. I used to live directly below a guy with an ageing prostate – his toilet bowl was right above my bed. When he pissed, it came in fits and starts, like a man squeezing water through a water pistol in sharp bursts. There would be a burst, and then a gap – obviously there would have been a big gap before the first burst, which, equally obviously, I never heard. During the piss, the gaps would get shorter, and the bursts more thunderous, reaching a peak of ten-second gaps, then petering out, with longer gaps and weaker bursts, and finally ending, a good half-minute after the final trickle, with a studied flush.

The guy's wife was quite different. In general she yelled a lot, and kept saying things like, 'I'm leaving you, Malcolm!' and 'I've already packed my bags, Malcolm'. Her orgasms were expressed with three or four increasingly loud shrieks, as if she were being jabbed with an electric cattle prod, rather than made love to by the penis of a man with an ageing prostate. When *she* pissed, it sounded like someone emptying a flagon of wine into the bowl; great volume and real consistency of flow.

26

I imagined this couple as a seventy-year-old and his chunky young concubine; a dirty old geezer and a young, vigorous woman. But they were both about thirty-five. The thing I wanted to say about my prostate, though, is that I sometimes feel a very slight squeezing pressure on my urethra, suggesting a slightly enlarged prostate. On the other hand, this is something I started feeling around twenty years ago, and might be my imagination. The real worry would be if I couldn't squeeze my prostate to shut off the flow.

Which I can.

It's at the back of my mind, this prostate thing. It worries me.

Right now, I don't have the heart to clean my teeth. Cleaning my teeth is a task that, these days, has no readily identifiable end. Of twenty-eight teeth, twelve remain unfilled, thirteen are filled, and three are crowns. Of the thirteen filled teeth, eight are more filling than tooth, shells really, cored out with a juddering drill and filled with either silver, or mercury-based amalgam, or white plastic stuff. These are all on the edge of needing to be crowns. The gaps between my teeth are inconsistent and contain snags, terrible toothpick traps, floss graveyards. And I'm worried about the mercury. Some say it's ageing, even carcinogenic.

If I were a horse or an elephant, I would be chewing in the last-chance saloon. These animals die when they run out of teeth. Horses have two sets of teeth. Elephants have six. When the final set wears down, and the teeth begin to fall out, the older elephant will move towards wet, marshy areas, in order to find food that needs less chewing. But I do not face this problem. For £10,000 I could go to a top dentist and have all my back teeth replaced with perfect, top-of-the-range crowns, and all my front ones whitened. My front ones are pretty good. That's the thing about me. I look okay on the surface, if you don't look too closely. The problem is the stuff *beneath* the surface. I'm like the *Titanic* in the hour or so after it hit the iceberg, but before it started sinking.

I know about the top dentist because I went to see him. It was a practice in a town house in wealthy north London. The dentist was a pristine man with a foreign accent. He took some X-rays, and then asked me to sit in his chair while he inspected my teeth with a pick and a mirror. There was a bit of scraping and tapping. Then I got out of the chair and sat at this guy's desk for the consultation.

He was appalled. My teeth, he said, were on the very edge of their natural lifespan.

My fillings were 'failing'.

I knew all about this. Because teeth rot from the outside, the holes caused by tooth decay are always largest on the surface of the tooth. This means that fillings are wedge-shaped, or cone-shaped. They are effectively chisels implanted into your teeth, struck many times each day by the hammers of the teeth above or below them. Eventually, a filling will split the tooth it is a part of, increasing the opportunity for new decay to enter. Small fillings lead to larger fillings. Eventually, there is not enough tooth left to fill. Then you have to have a crown.

I'm stressed, mostly because I'm falling apart, which makes me grind my teeth, which makes my teeth crumble, which makes me stressed, which makes me grind my teeth – Jesus, I'm doing it *now*.

Anyway. The top dentist told me he could clear my problems up. He could replace eight or ten teeth with crowns. Then the gaps between the crowns would be perfect. Flossing would be a pleasure, rather than the Pyrrhic victory it is now.

This sounded great.

Then he told me the price.

I went to a regular dentist. *He* told me my teeth were fine. Not exactly fine, but certainly workable. He would have to patch up

28

a few fillings. I might need a crown or two. It would be expensive.

'Expensive? How much?'

'£250, I'm afraid.'

So I went with the £250. Now I have no decay. But upkeep is a problem. It's like living in an old house; the woodwork has been painted over, rather than removed and replaced. And upkeep takes time. It takes more time every day.

I walk out of the bathroom, making a mental note to deal with my teeth later. Soon, I'll go back to the pristine dentist, and emerge, months later, with the teeth of a twenty-year-old – and, perhaps more importantly, with the gaps between the teeth of a twenty-year-old. Even sooner – sometime this morning, I suppose – I'll floss, pick, brush, gargle, rinse and spit. A lot of what I'll spit will be blood.

Like I said, it will be Pyrrhic.

But it will be a victory, of sorts.

Needing to cheer myself up, I decide to do a few minutes of Pilates. I turn the handle of the door that leads into my study – my office proper, the nerve centre of my operation. I'm hoping I'll be able to walk in and not feel a significant dip in my mood. Whenever I leave my study, it gets tidier in my imagination, returning eventually to an uncorrupted state, like Oscar Wilde's picture of Dorian Grey in reverse.

Actually stepping inside the room can be quite a shock.

Yesterday, on my walk, I passed a house and saw a flash of shelved books through the window, a sight that always interests me. I could see there was something not quite right, so I looked inside. Let me just say that one of my main fantasies, now that I'm middle-aged, is to live in a house with perfect bookshelves – crisp-looking shelves, painted white, shelves that contain all the books I want, that seem to be growing out of the walls, teeming yet tidy, a difficult balance to strike.

I'm forty-seven, and I want perfect shelves. This is not the fantasy I had as a ten-year-old, which was to play football professionally, and it's not my fifteen-year-old fantasy, which was to have sex, with more or less anybody, any female person that is, below the age of, I suppose, forty, and it's not my twenty-year-old fantasy, which was, in the course of an afternoon stroll, to meet several women blah blah, taking their clothes off blah blah. And it's not my thirty-year-old fantasy, which was again to play professional football. When I was thirty-one, I wrote a story on how a top sportsman – it was Gary Lineker – deals with the ageing process. He was just turning thirty himself. It struck me that sportsmen age at a more or less natural rate, as if they lived in the wild, like people in the Stone Age. In professional sport, a thirty-year-old is often referred to as a 'veteran'. That can hurt the middle-aged sports fan. You find yourself having to identify with the managers, and then, eventually, the owners.

Lineker moved like a sports star, which is to say like a young person, although he said that, between matches, he was often in pain. At thirty, he told me, recovery from the punishment of playing took much longer than it had even two or three years before. He said he felt stiff the day after a match. He felt bruised. He liked to have a lot of sleep in between matches. I asked him if he ever had a quick kickaround in the garden, and he said he did not.

In any case, I travelled with the England football team, and when we landed in the Czech Republic I walked down the steps of the small charter plane, and I was with the team, older than most of them, but not all of them, fatter than all of them, but not much fatter. This experience dug its way into my subconscious. I kept dreaming about it. In my dream, I was a footballer, on the pitch, in a big stadium, and I had the ball, and there was crowd noise, and I was being kicked in the ankles and the shins. That was the fantasy. The young man's pure excitement at being kicked.

Sixteen years ago I fantasised about being kicked, and now it's neat shelves I like. That's ageing for you. Now, if it was offered, I would subscribe to a magazine entitled *Bookshelf*, with pictures of people's bookshelves. I'd love that. Full-colour pictures of great shelves, printed on thick glossy paper. A good mix of book spines. Some old, some new. Some you've heard of, and some you've never heard of. Sometimes there would be other things on the shelves, like staplers or tiny Dictaphones.

So when I saw this shelf in the window, I crept closer. Something was not quite right. I put my hands around my face, in the shape of a diving mask, and peered into the window. Inside, it was horrible. The shelves were crammed, but books were lying diagonally, with other books on top of them, pressing their spines out of shape. Books had been piled on the floor, and now the piles were subsiding, like old ruins. A mound of books had silted up the area behind the desk, and was now climbing up the wall. Sheets of paper, with scribbled notes, were strewn on every surface. Around the desk, balls of paper had formed a nest. This was the study of a man in serious decline.

I went back to my office, to my home, to my paper-strewn nest, and started to tidy it up.

So the study is not as bad as it was. It is an illustration, using mostly wood-based materials, of the state of my mind. There are books in piles all over the top of my coffee table. The place is cluttered with books advising me how to get rid of clutter. There are piles of paper covered with notes, which will be filed, mostly unread, in special boxes, and then labelled, stacked in cup-boards, and never looked at again. These are *piles*. They are

31

not yet *mounds*. Piles always want to become mounds. I try not to let them.

For a moment, perhaps two or three seconds, something rattles or buzzes, a noise I do not recognise, and then it stops, and I wonder if it actually happened, if something, I can't think what, would rattle or buzz and then stop.

I lie on the floor, on a yoga mat, placing my radio next to me, and I suddenly feel the sensation that people describe as being 'like drowning' – a feeling of having the strength sucked away from me – although this is actually not anything like drowning. I know this, because I almost drowned once, and almost drowning, far from being a depressing experience, is exhilarating. When I almost drowned, I did not have the feelings of loss you'd normally associate with dying. It didn't feel like losing. It felt more like winning. It felt like being accelerated to the winning post. I was in the sea, standing in water up to my shoulders, and a current tugged at my feet and sucked me under, as if someone had tied a string to my feet and pulled on the string. I was churned around under the water. I was almost completely helpless. I was scraped along the sand. I was shot to the surface. The sea held me, and then expelled me. Then it pulled me back in again. I grabbed a breath here and there. I swallowed water. The whole thing felt like a giggling fit in which the thing you are giggling at, the sudden proximity of your own death, is much, much funnier than you thought it was. Being accelerated towards death has a lot in common with laughter – extreme danger, like a punchline, takes your thought processes on a whistle-stop tour of your unconscious. That's what people mean by 'your life flashing in front of your eyes'.

I remember the feeling of the water against my legs, and the loss of control, the total, absolute loss of control, and I remember being dragged and scraped, and I remember the water above me, and the

32

sight of the sky through the water, and then being pulled under again, being sucked along, tunnelling into the warmth.

Finally the surf spat me out on the beach. I was laughing hysterically, coughing and laughing, kneeling in the surf, water slapping my feet, not wanting the moment to end.

But what I feel now is the sensation that people *think* you have when you're drowning – I feel gloomy and lonely, sick with anxiety and dread.

I switch the radio on and twiddle the dial. Voices, on several wavelengths, tell me these things:

The market still looks poised to fall. Banks are suspending financial products – they are beginning to be worried about lending money. Deutsche Bank, a 'bellwether lender', has frozen its self-certified mortgages. In other words, no more lending to people who say they can afford it without being checked, a tipping point in any economic downturn.

One man says, 'How can the banks *not have known* they had so much liability?'

Also, there is a 'cancer epidemic'.

Exam results are the best ever.

The sport of competitive eating is growing exponentially, although its stars are now thin, rather than fat. They are people who take the sport seriously, not just greedy slobs. These new competitors have trained their digestive systems to process food at an ultra-fast rate.

An actor is awaiting sentence for being a pervert, leading to this speculation: the proportion of perverts, per head of population, is increasing.

And this competing speculation: pornography is increasing, thus flushing the already existing perverts out.

A four-year-old girl has been missing for more than three months.

The rich are getting richer, but more miserable, and the poor are getting richer, but more miserable. (Where is it all coming from, this money and this misery?)

Young black men are shooting and stabbing each other at an unprecedented rate.

Sportsmen are cheating. Testing them for drugs has no effect on the problem.

The weather seems to be getting more extreme. There has been flooding and drought. Experts say it's our fault. This last part is the real news, although here it's glossed over. We haven't thought of bad weather as being our fault since biblical times; I can't imagine what this is doing to our heads. (Incidentally, when I first saw the film *Magnolia*, which ends with a torrent of frogs falling from the sky, I thought this was a ridiculous scene to put in an otherwise serious film about the pain human beings mete out on each other. Now I like the frogs falling from the sky. Now I can see the point of the frogs falling from the sky.)

The Russians have planted a flag on the sea bed of the Arctic.

Bees are dying.

Trying to calm down, worried now about my chances of borrowing money at a reasonable rate, worried about the cancer epidemic, worried about guns, worried about the world my son will live in, which will be as unfamiliar to me as today's world is to my parents, I begin my Pilates exercises, placing two spiky balls under my buttocks and rolling around, massaging the muscles of my buttocks. I make a quick mental reckoning of the things that are good about my life. One: if my health complaints are minor – if I haven't got bowel cancer, if my mole is normal, if my liver has not been irreparably damaged, if I did not 'seed' lung or throat cancer when I smoked, if my prostate is not cancerous, and if the sharp, needling pains in

34

my head, neck and bowel can be explained by stress – then I might *just* be fine.

I am not fat.

I am no longer poisoning myself.

My fatigue, my terrible grinding tiredness, might not be because I'm ill, but simply because I'm building up sleep debts. The science writer Paul Martin in his book *Counting Sheep* says this is a classic symptom of middle age. Your sleep goes wrong. Which means your dreams go wrong. And, since your dreams are there to wash depression out of your brain, you get depressed. Which impacts further on your sleep. So my grinding fatigue, which knocks me flat in the middle of the day, might not be anything too bad. It might be *normal*.

Another good thing: more time off the booze might improve my liver function – hell, it *will* improve my liver function.

And: I can get my teeth done!

And my programme of two hours' brisk walking a day will gradually strengthen my heart, bringing my blood pressure down, so I will feel less frail and dizzy, and have less chance of keeling over with a stroke or a heart attack.

In fact, I might be fitter, and feel better, at fifty than I did at thirty-five.

I might get back together with the mother of my son (unlikely). Or I might fall in love with somebody else, as a healthy fifty-year-old, and things might work out, and my son could stay at weekends, and . . .

This gets complicated. My son might have to have a step-mother – or, worse, a step*father*. This makes me think of Richard Ford's character Frank Bascombe – poor, lonely Frank Bascombe, poor, lonely, divorced Frank Bascombe – who makes the point that children almost never think well of their father when their mother remarries, because he comes to be seen as

35

either a weakling or a bolter, a man who wasn't good enough, or one who thought himself too good.

And this, in turn, makes me think of another Bascombe pronouncement about one's passage through life.

When you're young, he says, your opponent is the future. But when you reach middle age, everything flips, and now you have a new opponent.

A far more powerful opponent.

The past.

Another good thing, and I feel the benefit of this every morning, is that I did not smoke any cigarettes last night. When I applied for life insurance, my financial adviser asked me when I'd last smoked a cigarette, and I said that, although I'd been a non-smoker for ages, I did smoke part of a cigarette a few months ago, 'around the Christmas period'. He told me it was important to admit this on the form, and that they had very accurate testing devices, and also that, if I was caught out in a lie, the ramifications would be huge. Nobody would ever trust me again, basically. So I admitted it, along with the fact that I'd been a drug user in the past – cannabis, cocaine and ecstasy, I said. Anyway, part of a cigarette smoked six months ago makes me, in insurance terms, a smoker, so I'll have to pay smokers' premiums until twelve months have passed since I inhaled any tobacco, which makes my half-cigarette a costly blunder, to the tune of £180.

Still, I can see their point. Smoking is, for most people, hell to give up, and if you've done it a bit in the last year, you're likely, at some point, to do it a lot more. I didn't find it hard to stop, I think because I always saw myself as a non-smoker who sometimes smoked, rather than as a smoker. Smoking was something I'd done when I was young; in a way, it defined young adulthood, the period when you can try on different identities, knowing you have time to re-invent yourself.

At some point in my thirties, smoking made me feel, not younger, but older – holding a cigarette made me feel self-conscious. I didn't want to be seen doing it. I thought that if people saw me do it, at my age, they'd pity me. Also, I knew what it was doing – it prematurely ages the cells of your throat and lungs, and the cells of the insides of your cheeks, your tongue, and your gums, and the cells of the skin around your mouth and eyes. When you look at an older smoker's mouth, it looks all crabby and wrinkled, and that's because the toxins in the smoke have caused the skin cells to go through so many repair cycles that they've begun to make mistakes.

But of the 25 or so per cent of smokers who get cancer of the mouth, throat, oesophagus or lungs, the overwhelming majority are twenty/twenty smokers – people who have smoked at least twenty cigarettes a day for twenty years or more – a total of 150,000 or 200,000 cigarettes. These are the cancer numbers. I smoked maybe five or ten cigarettes a day for around thirteen years – between the ages of nineteen and twenty-six, and again between the ages of thirty-four and forty, less than 20,000 cigarettes in all. But I still had horrible symptoms when I did it, including strange pains in the left side of my throat, a feeling of lung blockage and a wet cough. I also had what the anti-smoking guru Allen Carr termed 'black shadows' – guilty feelings at the back of my mind, fears I did not dare to confront.

If I had my time again I would still smoke and still quit in my mid-twenties, but I would not start again in my thirties. I think I came fairly close to a lifetime of being a non-smoker who smokes, which would have meant smoking another 30,000 cigarettes, possibly enough to tip the balance, if not towards cancer, then towards something else, possibly a stroke or heart disease. But something made me stop, so I hardly smoked at all in my forties, and now the black shadows have almost gone. Now I can't imagine what life would be like, how frightening it would be, if I did not feel cushioned by the fact that I no longer smoke. In this way, not smoking has become more addictive in middle age than smoking ever was in youth.

But I still worry – 200,000 inhaled mouthfuls of smoke, over two periods lasting half a decade each. It's a significant part of my past.

But is it indelible?

Would it show up on a scan?

Did I get away with it?

When you quit smoking, the only real problem is that you think it's always going to be as bad as it is in the first few days, which makes you want to start again, so you start again, thus reinforcing the cycle. Allen Carr's key point is that it's smoking that makes you want to smoke, which means that at some point after you quit smoking, you won't want to smoke, because you don't smoke. The key to quitting, in other words, is the belief that the future will not be like the present. And this is a bit like what happens when a relationship ends. You think it's always going to feel this bad. But it won't. That's what you have to tell yourself.

It won't.

That's what you have to say.

Things will get better.

It will be easy – as easy as quitting smoking.

Will I die a smoking-related death? Both of my grandfathers did. My father's father died of emphysema, a condition in which the alveoli, the tiny sacs that make up the pulp of your lungs, become less elastic – less like balloons and more like, say, old suede shoes. The process is roughly as follows. The smoke irritates the tissues of the alveoli. Thinking they are under viral or bacterial attack, the alveoli release their own attack dogs, enzymes called proteases, to maul the attacking viruses or germs.

At this point, the alveoli are not worried about being mauled themselves, because they never usually let the dogs out without strict instructions – maul the viruses, or the germs, they say, but not us. These instructions are carried out by a protein called alpha-l-antitrypsin. But the smoke, as well as irritating the sacs, also blocks the release of the protein. So the dogs never get the instructions. So the sacs are not only irritated, but also mauled by the dogs.

And now, with all this irritation and mauling, the cells of the sacs need to be constantly repaired – and repair, after many repetitions, stops being perfect. The result of this imperfect repair is that the sacs lose their elasticity. This, in turn, means that when they fill up with air, they can't expel it as quickly as they could before, so that, even when the air becomes de-oxygenated and stale, it still hangs around. So the sacs are now like old suede shoes, full of stale air, which stops the good air from getting in. They also release mucus, and the mucus further blocks the airways. So now you're trying to suck air into an old shoe, already full of stagnant, putrid gas, which is also filling up with snot and phlegm.

And this, of course, makes your heart work harder, because the whole point of breathing is to get oxygen into your blood, via your lungs, so that the blood can take oxygen to your tissues. After, say, 100,000 cigarettes – say a million lungfuls of smoke – the elastic sphere of every alveolus has turned into a crusty snot-shoe, and you have to work very hard to suck air through the snot-shoe and into your blood, so it follows that you strain your heart. Also, of course, your tissues are now living on stale, snotty air, rather than the clean air you breathed before.

Incidentally, emphysema is what would happen to your lungs even if you didn't smoke. It's a consequence of the ageing process. If you lived to the age of 120, and nothing else was wrong with you, you'd probably die of emphysema. That's because there are lots of irritants other than tobacco smoke in the air – your alveoli will always need to repair themselves, and will always harden, always fill up with stale air. At 120, they would probably become snot-shoes even if you didn't smoke. With my grandfather, this process was accelerated. By the age of sixty he was wheezing, and twenty years later he was in serious trouble. At eighty-three, he entered hospital for the last time. I remember one of my parents telling me he was breathing out of the very tops of his lungs. He died a few painful, vomity weeks later. I was sixteen, and just beginning to smoke.

Strange – I saw no connection between my grandfather's snot-shoe lungs and my own smoking. At thirteen or fourteen I had smoked leaves and grass, just ordinary grass, packed into the hollow stalks of plants, which was disgusting, absolutely disgusting, but that was not the point. It was smoking. That was the point. The thought that smoking might be pleasant, or even addictive, would have seemed too good to be true. You put up with the horrors in order to smoke – that was the order of things. And then, much later, you discovered that tobacco was less disgusting than purely random bits of plant matter. Later still, you 'got' tobacco. And then you liked it. And then you didn't like not having it.

After a while, you understand that you shouldn't smoke, because you can feel the beginnings of the damage it's doing. But you also know that you are young, that there is still time to quit without the damage being significant. If you smoke until you're twenty-five, for instance, you might have knocked twenty years off the potential life of your lungs. But that would still mean your lungs could last into your nineties; another organ would almost certainly fail first.

Smoking is a young person's thing. You smoke because you are young. But, at some crucial point, you begin to feel that you are young because you smoke. You begin to feel that smoking *makes* you young. That to stop smoking would be to stop being young. Your logic gets twisted. Part of you thinks: how can I stop smoking? It would age me terribly.

I never went to see my father's father in hospital. My parents wanted to protect us – both him and me – from the unpleasantness of this situation. Can you imagine the shame of that? You are dying, but, because you smoked, and because your smoking has given you the lungs of a man of 120, and because this makes you cough up pus and blood, you cannot see your grandson. After he died, there were only four people at his funeral – my father, myself, and a man and a woman we'd never met – people who'd been his neighbours briefly. My mother and brother stayed behind with my grandmother, who, for reasons I never fathomed, refused to go. She was eighty-three, and looked to be on the way out. In fact, she would live for another decade and a half.

My father and I and the two strangers took a taxi to the church, in a part of west London we did not know. It was a hot day. We were sweltering in our suits. When we arrived at the church, it was locked. Nobody was around. My father checked that we'd come to the right place. We had. The time for the funeral came and went. We waited in the churchyard. My father went off to phone my mother. Then he came back. After about an hour of waiting, the verger appeared, on his rounds.

My father talked to the verger.

The verger said something like: '*Oh* no. He's done this before.'

The vicar had forgotten about the funeral. That was the bad news. But there was good news. The coffin was probably in the church. The verger didn't see why not – it had to be in there. He went in, and came out, and, sure enough, there was a coffin in there. The verger went away and fixed things up – he called another vicar, who did a slightly casual service, sort of like aircrew running through the safety procedures when there are only a couple of people on the plane.

There was no music.

I wondered, and still wonder, how long he'd have lived if he hadn't smoked, and I suppose I have an answer of sorts – his older brother, who did not smoke, died at the age of ninety-six. Their mother had been 101.

And I also wonder about my mother's father, whose dead face I saw, and did not recognise, the night before his funeral. *He* died, of a massive stroke, at the age of seventy-seven. This is not strictly true – he was starved to death, in hospital, by doctors and nurses, having been in a coma for eleven weeks, after a massive stroke, which itself followed a smaller stroke the day before, which itself followed an even smaller stroke eighteen months before that.

After the first stroke, doctors advised my grandfather to stop smoking and drinking. He smoked forty cigarettes a day, and drank probably six beers every evening. His smoking style seemed disinterested, automatic – not the hungry bolting down of gobs of smoke as practised by my father's father. But my mother's father was always smoking, from the first cigarette in the morning after breakfast – the 'shit-trigger', as some people call it – to the cigarette he smoked after he came back from the pub, and before he fell into his snore-racked sleep at around midnight. So this was not *always* smoking – in fact, he smoked a cigarette, which took him about six minutes, every twenty-five minutes.

So he smoked 24 per cent of the time.

His problem was high blood pressure. True, he had snot-shoe lungs, although not as crusty as those of my father's father. His cough was wet, rather than constricted and tight. Also true, he had many symptoms of alcohol abuse – a florid face, probable liver damage, digestive trouble, and, almost certainly, mild dementia. But what killed him was an ischaemic stroke – a blocked artery in the brain – and what caused the stroke was the formation of plaque on another artery. Plaques are caused by the body's inability to deal with molecules of fat known as LDL cholesterol, which look like the spiky balls you massage your bottom with when you do Pilates. Young bodies can store this cholesterol in their cells. Older bodies can't. Gerontologists think there's a link between sex hormones and the ability to store LDL cholesterol. Around the time you begin to lose your sex drive, the spiky balls can't be stored, so they bash into the walls of your arteries, causing scar tissue to form. These scars turn into plaques.

And what happens when you have plaques in your arteries? The arteries become narrower. That's why you get high blood pressure. Think of what happens when you partially cover the end of a garden hose. The water coming through the hose comes through at greater pressure, doesn't it? When this happens to your blood, all the little spiky balls get fired at the artery walls with more force, causing bigger lesions, which in turn cause a build-up of more scar tissue. So the lesions get bigger. They begin to snag platelets, clot-forming agents in the blood. My mother's father had snot-shoe lungs, an overworked heart, high blood pressure, switched-off sex hormones (when was the last time he ever 'bothered' my grandmother? The late 1960s?), too many spiky balls in his blood, and a gardener's thumb over the end of his hose, and, after a while, a lesion in one of his arteries must have snagged a lump of platelets, and the gardener's-thumb effect must have knocked it loose, at which point the lump, or clot, must have travelled deep into his brain, and become wedged in an artery.

That was stroke number one. He lost the movement in the left side of his body. His face drooped. But he began to recover. After a month, his face was back to normal; after three months, he could walk again, and after six months, he appeared to be fine, almost as if nothing had happened. That was when his doctor told him not to drink or smoke, and he didn't. Then he recovered. I remember visiting my grandparents a little less than a year after his stroke, and being surprised by two things – the extent of his recovery, and the fact that he was drinking and smoking again. He explained it to me. 'The doctor,' he said, 'told me I if I started again, I might only have a year or two left. So I started again.'

A year or two, a year or two of his old life, of going out drinking every night, had seemed like a long time.

Actually, he got about another nine months. Then he had two strokes in one day. The first paralysed him, more or less totally. The second put him in a coma, from which he never woke up, although, sitting beside him in the hospital, I wondered if he wasn't conscious of what was going on around him. He seemed to be in a permanently bad mood. He didn't look happy. He looked restless and grumpy. He did not talk or open his eyes, but, if you squeezed his hand, he sometimes squeezed it back. The nurse said he'd probably die of an infection after a week or two. They nearly always get an infection, she said, and usually die of it, and, sure enough, he got a chest infection, but he rode it out – he was the Germans at dawn on 6 June 1944 – and in the end they had to starve him to death, and after that, the next time I saw him he was in his coffin, looking pale and unlined, creepily like he had in photographs taken in the 1920s. His brother, who smoked heavily, died in his sixties, of lung cancer. His sisters, who did not smoke, died at the ages of ninety-three and ninety-seven.

His wife, my maternal grandmother, died of leukaemia twelve years later, at the age of eighty-eight. She was diagnosed at the

44

age of eighty-two and doctors had got the leukaemia under control by the time she was eighty-four. 'She'll die of something else,' they said. But then she was knocked down in the street by a drunken driver, at the age of eighty-six, and she broke her hip in the fall, and after that the leukaemia overpowered her. Her body was able to repair her hip, but only at great expense.

My other grandmother, the one who hadn't gone to her husband's funeral, broke one hip in her late eighties, and then she broke her other hip in her early nineties. Both times, doctors told us that she would almost certainly not recover. But both times she did recover. She had no cancer and no vascular problems. Her arteries had almost certainly lost some elasticity, but had almost certainly not formed dangerous plaques. Her cholesterol was fine. By the time she was ninety-five, she was weak, but nothing was killing her. At ninety-seven, she was bedridden, but still nothing was killing her. People visited her every day to make sure she didn't get bedsores – wounds caused by simple friction. But she did get bedsores, and the bedsores became infected. In the end, as she approached the age of ninety-eight, her ability to repel the infection failed.

I went to see her on the day she died. She was lying in bed, hardly moving, with her eyes closed. We had this joke routine, me and my grandmother. She would hold out her thumb, and try to push my thumb away, and I'd jump backwards and say how strong she was. In my twenties, I would actually throw myself to the floor. I stopped doing this when I was about twenty-five, when she was about ninety-two. Now I was thirty, and she was nearly ninety-eight. She had about an hour to live. Just before I left, she raised her thumb. I pushed it, and moved back slightly. I did not jump backwards. Neither of us said much. I said something, but I can't remember what it was. She tried to smile, but could not. I tried to smile, but could not.

45

On the way out, I said, 'See you', pretty sure, even then, that I was lying.

My grandparents died, respectively, of emphysema, stroke, leukaemia and infection – on one level, four quite different things. But on another level, they died of a very similar thing – the inability of their cells to perform endless repairs. Or, more complicatedly, the inability of their cells' DNA to repeat the same instructions endlessly. 'Do this, and this, and this,' says the DNA in each cell, like a digital computer program. And everything is fine, through millions of repetitions. And then, one day, something is not fine. One day, the instructions are slightly different. Mistakes start happening. As with the Germans on the bluff above Omaha Beach, mistakes beget mistakes.

And, as I can see in the mirror, after I've completed my Pilates exercises, shakily pulled my clothes on, and splashed water on my face, I have a groove in the middle of my forehead, and fine lines in the corners of my eyes.

My cells, too, have started to make mistakes.

This is what I'm thinking about as I walk down the stairs and out into the street, as I buy my newspapers, and as I walk towards the nearest café, five minutes down the street. Bits of me have started to make mistakes.

I'm patting my pockets, worried I've lost something or left something behind, also running through a mental checklist of things I might not have switched off or locked, and I run through this checklist another time, and another, and I tell it to stop, to go away, to just . . . go away.

Some good news: my fever is settling down. Perhaps it will progress gently, hang around for a while, and bow out.

Or perhaps it is biding its time, waiting to strike.

Some bad news: perhaps the tissue pain and fatigue that seemed, twenty minutes ago, to be the start of a fever, might not be a fever at all. It might be normality. It might be that this is just how I'm supposed to feel on a grimly ordinary morning, at this stage of my life.

In the café I order a double espresso and rub my temples, trying to ease the mild stabbing sensations inside my head. My newspaper lies unopened on the table in front of me.

My newspaper.

I'm thinking about the fact that when my cells repair my tissues, they do so by reproducing copies of their own DNA – the blueprint, or instruction manual, for my body. This DNA has been described as an encyclopaedia. But another way of looking at it, I now see, is as a newspaper – a daily newspaper that must be published every day, in each of my cells, just to keep my body going. But it's not a normal newspaper, which, like the ones on my table, must be different every day.

This is a newspaper that must be *exactly the same* every day.

Imagine the pressure on the staff. You have to produce the newspaper every day, and it must be the same in every minute detail. The stories must be the same. The headlines must be the same. The ink must be exactly as bold as it was yesterday, exactly as bold as it will be tomorrow. Every day, in the editorial conference, the editor will sit behind his desk and criticise the staff. He will notice things. Even if there are not mistakes, he will explain that this is only because of the vigilance of one man – himself.

Sometimes, the editor will appear in one of the newspaper's departments, to give the staff an impromptu talk. He will talk generally for a while – about targets, about successes and failures, about the importance of vigilance. He will creep around the building, muttering. Everybody involved in the newspaper will come to believe that their job is on the line.

47

Sometimes, a dark cloud will descend over the editor, and he will go out for a long lunch with a close colleague – the sports editor, say – and the two men, paranoid and portly, will come back to the office, and some dark magic will have been worked on them. One of them will start shouting, bellowing, at one or more of his colleagues. Egos will be bruised. Staff will sit, heads down, brows furrowed over notes, fingers tapping keyboards.

The pressure, people will say. The pressure's getting to him.

But the newspaper will come out, every day. And every day, it will be the same as it was the day before.

And one day, the newspaper's owner will arrange a meeting with the editor in the boardroom, a big room at the top of the building with a long, pale table running the length of the room. It's bad news, he will say. Mistakes have been spotted. So far, he'll point out, we seem to have got away with it.

Little does he know that, once the rot has started, it never stops, that when DNA replicates, it loses part of itself each time.

In the human body, DNA is designed in strands, with spare bits at the end of each strand. These spare bits are known as telomeres. But they don't last for ever. It's as if you have a reservoir of ink to print your newspaper with. One day, the ink looks faint. Another day, it runs out.

Think of the telomeres as ink. Eventually, they get used up.

When this happens, your manuscript is corrupted. The instructions for repairing your cells become harder to read. So your cells start to look different. They get denser and thicker, less elastic.

Your daily newspaper becomes brasher and more vulgar. You become a tabloid version of yourself. Your elegant leader columns are replaced with pages of knee-jerk opinions, recycled old wives' tales, horoscopes, celebrity bitching, xenophobia, lists of trivia and gross pictures of Britney Spears' bottom.

*   *   *

48

Waiting for my coffee, I notice in one of my tabloids that Britney Spears' bottom appears to have hairs growing out of it, although this might be stray tendrils of ink. The caption tells me that she's been 'giving onlookers an eyeful of her peachy bum'.

It's stray ink.

Not hairs.

And there's a debate about Jack Nicholson's flesh, which is sagging, and Vladimir Putin's, which is not so bad. One woman says she prefers Putin, because his youthful torso gives the impression of a man in control. A rival columnist says that she, on the other hand, prefers Nicholson, because his ageing torso shows that he knows how to have fun. Nicholson looks dreadful, really puffy, but I definitely admire the fact that he seems unworried about it, and I try to imagine what he really feels like – possibly he's so old now that he doesn't mind – and I think of a conversation I had the other day with another guy in his forties, about getting old, and what suddenly jumped into my mind was the idea that your fortysomething decade is the worst possible age, because you feel like a failed young person, whereas in your fifties you might feel like rather a sprightly older person, having cruised past the awkward phase of being a failed young person. And when I said this the other guy nodded, and we laughed, and I walked on, thinking about how I might be able to cope with being in my forties in a few years' time, when I'm into my fifties.

If I get into my fifties.

Which makes me think about Jimmy, the fifty-year-old busker I chat to on my walks, who looks about seventy. He's drunk for most of each day, and smokes fifty or sixty cigarettes; his few remaining teeth are rotten, he has bags under his eyes and deep crevasses in his rhino-like facial skin. He's thin, he eats poorly – I wonder how he even got to be fifty. The other day he told me that he'd been vomiting at night, and finding it increasingly hard to swallow, so he went to see the doctor.

Cancer of the gullet. That's what the doc had thought. So Jimmy spent yesterday in hospital with a camera down his throat.

I wonder if I'll see him again.

And I look up, at the light outside, at the cars outside, I look away from my newspaper, and I think about Jimmy, and if I had a chance to bet on it, I'd bet he had cancer, and I open my newspaper to another page, and I wonder if things really are getting worse, or if it's just me having a mid-life crisis.

I'm still thinking about this when my coffee arrives.

Chapter 2

Twenty minutes later, having drunk two cups of coffee, having read the newspapers, I'm heading out of the café on my first walk of the day. I will walk along the river, past the big supermarket with its Alpine cupola, and then across the bridge and back through the little shopping precinct. Or maybe I'll do it the other way around, starting with the precinct, the plaza of cheap shoes and cheap medicines and the two health stores which, it seems to me, are starting to be sweet shops disguised as health stores, the fruit and nuts retreating to the back of the store, while the chocolate-covered goodies move towards the front. But this might be my imagination. I'm paranoid lately, and the coffee has made me edgy.

I'm holding my newspapers, rolled up into a baton.

I'm walking briskly.

I'm marching.

I hope that, if I get my body going, I will feel a rush of endorphins, and this will help. It might dislodge the headache that, I know now, is beginning to settle behind my eyes. A walk might chase away the latent fever, the viral load lurking in my muscles, awaiting its moment. A walk will relax me. Relaxed, my brain might begin to work a little better, and I might not fall apart when I see the mother of my little boy, and my little boy might not see me struck dumb, or else mumbling like an idiot, mumbling and panicking and making no sense.

Is it panicking that I do? Or is it choking? Choking is the opposite of panicking. I'm trying to remember an article I read about those two types of brain malfunction, which, I believe, become more common as we age. Old people can panic, or choke, at the slightest thing, especially under stress, like my grandmother after she was knocked down by the drunken driver. The car, not speeding, but slightly weaving, hit her at mid-thigh, and she broke her hip when she hit the kerb. Her bones were brittle. She was taken to hospital in an ambulance. Her hip was set, using metal pins. But then she woke up in the middle of the night, and, seeing a hospital orderly, and believing herself to be in bed, in her house, she concluded that she had been burgled, and that the burglar had somehow tied her up, using plastic IV cords and a saline drip, which she ripped out, before somehow getting out of bed and falling again. Later, when she understood what had happened, understood that she'd been knocked down in the street by a drunken driver and taken to hospital, she still believed that, once there, she'd been kid-napped and tied up, and that she had escaped. For days, she panicked, or choked, at the sight of certain orderlies, certain nurses, and when I visited her, she kept telling me the story of the kidnap, telling me that it had happened, that she was worried it might happen again, and that nobody believed her.

'You believe me, don't you?'

'Uh-huh,' I said.

The hip healed. But the hip was not the problem. The leukaemia, which had been brought under control, and which then raged out of control, was the problem. Healing the hip overloaded the system; it was too much. Healing the hip gave the leukaemia a chance, gave it a clear run, gave it defilade. The leukaemia was like Tom Hanks hiding behind the concrete bunker, waiting for something to go wrong, waiting for the Germans to lose concentration.

In the end, my grandmother was the Germans.

In the end, we are all the Germans.

Ah yes – some of the fog in my mind is clearing. I can remember the article about panicking and choking. When I remember things – a slower process now, at forty-seven, than when I was, say, thirty-seven – I call them up, metaphorically speaking, on a mental screen and look at them. When I was younger, I could read a book – say, *Rogue Trader* by the disgraced investment banker Nick Leeson – and, if somebody asked me something about the book, I would mentally flip through the pages, which would appear, slightly more blurred and incomplete than the real thing, but still there, and sometimes I could remember where in the book I'd read the relevant passage. I remember explaining to somebody the process by which Leeson managed to lose so much money, and why the expanding debt was analogous to the way cancer grows in a body, and, as I said this, I sat there, mentally flipping the pages, until I saw the relevant passage, towards the top of a right-hand page. The passage was about how Leeson had bypassed the normal system of checks and balances, and I'd read something similar about how cancer starts on the cellular level.

I was forty-two.

I can do this now, but not as well as I could, and, as I'm pondering this loss, and feeling a stab of sadness because of it, I decide to take the river path.

The article about panicking and choking was written by Malcolm Gladwell. It's coming back to me now. I read it in the garden of a pub the day I went to see a dentist several years ago. How many years? My instinct says four, but my instinct, these days, estimates low. So maybe five or six years ago. As this memory returns, colours appear, emotions, smells. It was a hot day in August. A nice pub in a nasty part of town. An oasis of gentrification. Some kind of gloopy sauce with my lunch. Later, I went back home to the place below the bathroom of the man with the faulty prostate.

According to Gladwell, panicking is what happened when John Kennedy Junior crashed his plane – anxiety robbed him of the ability to think in a straight line. Choking, on the other hand, is what Jana Novotná did when she threw away the Wimbledon Ladies' title in the early 1990s. She was winning 4–1 in the second set, having won the first. She was serving for the game, which would have made it 5–1. And then she started 'choking' – thinking too much, retreating from intuition, unable to trust her instinctive brain. When you choke, you think in a stilted way. You force the brain to use main channels, rather than the usual mixture of main channels and tributaries, and you do this because you're afraid of getting lost.

This is what I do when I see the mother of my little boy.

I choke.

Now I'm remembering the article. In my memory, the magazine comes into focus. I'm seeing the typesetting, the way it was positioned on the octagonal wooden table, the table slatted, the magazine unfurling slightly on the slatted table because I had carried it across town rolled up in a baton . . .

Can this be right?

I'm holding today's newspapers rolled up in a baton, too.

I stride on, holding today's baton. It contains the woes of the world, stories about guns, about young people with guns, about the nervous market, about this year's good exam results, which are the result of a con, a Ponzi scheme, and which, therefore, are not good exam results. They are bad exam results. The baton tells me about the death of love and the end of sport, and the baton asks why.

The baton does not know.

The baton does not really want to know.

The coffee has made me waspish and edgy. But the endorphins from walking are starting to make me loose and relaxed. A perfect combination, you might think. It's like a speedball, the heroin to make you loose and the cocaine to perk you up – I was going to say a poor man's speedball, but that's not what I mean.

I don't do drugs now.

Now I do my 15,000 steps every day.

Now I'm marching along, towards the river and the supermarket, with its Alpine cupola, passing the specialist underwear outlet, holding the baton that contains the woes of the world.

'Why?' says the baton.

But the baton does not want to know. Everything falling apart, kids with guns, banks not able to explain where their money's gone, house prices crazy, monogamy on its last legs, levels of unhappiness soaring, levels of clinical depression off the scale, graffiti everywhere, perverts looming, children missing. What was it Joan Didion said? The centre is not holding, that's right – the centre is not holding, a quote from somebody, Yeats I think, not sure but I think it's Yeats, Didion writing about the San Francisco of 1967, telling us about the coldness and alienation that went along with the sex and drugs, and now things are the same apart from one detail, which is that the coldness and alienation have a corporate feel, and my instinct here is to say that things should be fine, but they're not, things should be fine, but we're not happy, really not happy at all, when you think about the fact that we're so incredibly comfortable it seems weird that we're not happy, but our comfort comes at a price, it comes at a high price. There's something murky and wrong about our way of life, something shifty and treacherous, and we can feel it, can't we, and it's beginning to tell, things are starting to give, things are starting to run out. We're eating away at the seed capital. We're using up the telomeres. We can't go on doing things the way we're doing them, can't borrow any more, can't write any more cheques. These are the woes of the world.

'Why?' says the baton.

But the baton does not really want to know.

And as I march along, approaching Bobby, who is a heroin-addict-turned-alcoholic sitting on a bench, sunning his wide red face – as I march along, I toss the baton into a bin, it spins satisfyingly and lands on the pile of dog shit the riverside dog walkers have been considerate enough to put into plastic bags. Shit in plastic – a greater environmental headache, I would have thought, than shit *per se*. Tell me I'm wrong.

'All right?' says Bobby.

'Yourself?' I say.

Bobby takes a swig of organic beer, bought from the organic produce shop that opens early. Recently, I went in there to buy some ingredients for my anti-ageing porridge, and the woman who owns the place told me somebody had found a body along the river bank, a man my age, fortysomething, who'd died of a heroin overdose, and I immediately thought of Bobby. But he was sitting on the bench as usual, tipping his big squarish head back and emptying a can of lager into his throat. So it wasn't him. But he'd been there. He told me the story, which involved a relapse into heroin on his part, having been led astray, as he described it, by another guy. There was the struggle to find a vein, some pretty disgusting stuff about the other guy's scabs, and then the other guy's death. Bobby described it in terms of not knowing what to do, and my memory of his description has the scabby guy keeling over, the scabby guy dying, and Bobby panicking, finding the scabby guy's girlfriend, then being quizzed by the police.

(I thought: 'The scabby guy had a *girlfriend*? And I get dumped?')

Now we talk about drinking. I stand, hands on hips, the smug ex-drinker, while Bobby tells me he doesn't drink very much.

He says, 'You've stopped, haven't you?'

'Yup.'

He's forty-five, and still has his teeth, unlike Jimmy the busker. He is not skinny either – drink still puts weight on him. He has hepatitis C, from dirty needles.

Bobby takes another swig. 'My doctor tells me I shouldn't do it,' he says as I start to walk off. 'And that's why I only have the odd one, like.'

What I can't get out of my mind is the fact that everything ends, everything dies, absolutely without exception – every society, for instance. *Every* society dies. Every TV series dies. Every person. And I've been trying to understand the essential reason for it. If everything dies, there must be a reason.

For instance, this Alpine cupola up ahead of me, designed so you can see the supermarket from miles away, from the tops of hills even, this cupola will, one day, be rubble; archaeologists will find bits of it and add it to their skimpy collection of evidence, piecing together the twenty-first-century Western lifestyle. One day, five hundred years from now, somebody will reconstruct a super-market, from sandwich fridge to cupola, and amaze people with stories of 20,000 products under one roof, vegetables flown in from all over the world, cheap meat, and racks of glossy magazines depicting famous people as if they were animals in a zoo.

At this early hour, the supermarket does not have the newly minted feel of a café or produce store first thing in the morning – it already seems tired, tired and washed-out and old, the car park mostly empty, stray trolleys at the edges, a couple of pale smokers pacing outside. There are two people in the café, both

57

in the uniform of the supermarket, recycling their wages into bacon sandwiches and cups of coffee.

I won't go in. I'll bear left, the river at my left side. Rising up on the other side is the hill I'll climb later, when I go to see my little boy. Looking up at the hill, I am filled with a looming sense of hope.

Maybe things will work out.

Maybe we'll get back together, my little boy's mother and me. It's *possible*.

Maybe, if I turn into the person I might have turned into, rather than being the person I did turn into – maybe if I stop dreaming and procrastinating, if I 'turn the corner'. Maybe, if Freud, who thought our minds were pretty much set in stone by the age of forty-five, was wrong, and Jung, who thought that we are capable of great change in later life, was right . . . maybe things *will* work out. Maybe, in a year's time, all of this will seem like a bad dream. I lived in my office for a while, I will say, but then we patched things up.

Maybe if I buy my house, if I can get a mortgage, if the lender looks kindly on me, if I can get life insurance. Maybe if I become part of society, a joiner, rather than hanging around the edges, carping.

And suddenly I see my problem; I'm a waster, a has-been, a person who has used up most of his resources. I'm past my peak. Unless Jung was right, and Freud was wrong. But if you apply the principle of Occam's razor – look at the alternatives, and go for the simplest, most obvious one – I think Freud was right. Jung was nuts, anyway.

I'm a waster.

I'm finished.

Christ, I haven't even got my career going properly, and now I'm seventeen years away from retirement age. I'm forty-seven! How bad, how *embarrassing*, is that?

58

I watched a TV programme recently, caught a few minutes of it, about a man and his wife looking for a second home. They were walking along the beach in Bermuda. The guy explained how he'd planned for early retirement, saved his money, was due a fat pension. He'd worked in the public sector and wasn't particularly rich, just careful and sensible. Just not a waster. Now he had a couple more years to go, and that was that. He was my age, give or take a few months, and looking forward to retiring at fifty. He'd started work at sixteen. He got in early.

I approached life the other way around – left school at eighteen, and took a year off, with the intention of bumming around. I didn't want to work at all – I wanted to go on the dole and do absolutely nothing. But my parents insisted I work. Their idea was that work was good – work benefited the community. I did not believe it. I certainly don't believe it now. I think work, for the most part, actually *hurts* people, and hurts the world. Work is also inflationary – people are working longer hours than ever before, which earns them more money, which causes prices to go up. We're caught in a work spiral, as explained in that book, I can see it now, can picture it in my mind – yes, *Willing Slaves*, by Madeleine Bunting. Madeleine, the same name as the missing girl. I keep noticing Madeleines all over the place now, they seem to be coming out of the woodwork, and of course it's because of the missing girl. Thinking about this, about missing children, lost children, causes a bubble to expand in my chest, and then burst, my synapses firing panic signals across my brain, with blood being rerouted from the stomach into my muscles, putting me on alert, just in case.

Anyway, Madeleine Bunting says we're caught in a work spiral. But then we're caught in all sorts of other spirals, too – a traffic spiral, a self-esteem spiral, a celebrity spiral, a luxury spiral. Yes, a luxury spiral. It's a trick, of course, an elaborate illusion. Luxuries used to be scarce things, but then people caught on to the idea that luxuries could be anything, as long as they were expensive. And then another stage – luxuries could be anything, as long as they appeared to be expensive. Now, we are living in the endgame – apparent luxuries have become necessities, and the people who make them run such highly geared businesses that they have to sell more apparent luxuries all the time just to keep afloat, and if they went under we'd all go under. Imagine what that's doing to our heads – the entire economy based on the selling of illusions. I heard somebody on the radio the other day explaining that, in order not to ruin the planet with carbon emissions, we'd have to stop freighting things around in trucks, and start freighting them around on trains instead. That was his solution, God help us. Not a thought in his head of stopping the freight altogether, stopping the madness. Too late for that, my friend.

What has happened to us?

To be happy, a Stone Age family needed food and shelter. Fifty years ago, it was food, shelter, hot and cold running water and good crockery for special occasions. Now you have to have designer labels, sexual allure and fame; that's what people want these days. To be happy, you have to work harder and harder just to stay still. That's what Madeleine Bunting found when she researched the topic.

What I think is this: work is not the solution. Work is the problem.

Work ages the planet.

When I was eighteen I had absolutely no idea about work – the sheer grinding dullness of it, the way it made time creep and hobble along, so that at lunchtime you can't believe the whole day isn't over. My first job was writing government cheques to the relatives of people who had died, and also to people who had chronic illnesses. I wrote a cheque to a Mrs Dedman, because her husband, Mr Dedman, had died, and I showed it to people, thinking it was funny, but nobody thought it was funny. They had seen every kind of name. They had seen it all.

Each time you wrote a cheque you had to go through a whole list of information. It wasn't just writing cheques. It was a whole complicated business. For instance, if you went to get a cup of tea from the tea trolley, you had to lock your cheques in a special drawer. You weren't allowed to let them out of your sight, in case the other people at your desk stole them. On my third day, I was given a message to see the boss of my office, Mr Webb. He'd had a report that I'd been to the tea trolley without locking my cheques in my drawer. He said he'd 'have to let me go' if it happened again.

I can see him now, the old time-server, hair parted at the side and greying at the temples, creases between his nose and mouth, *nasolabial folds*; I can see him now, in his office, his small office, telling me he'd have to let me go if I didn't lock my cheques up in my drawer when I went to the tea trolley. I can see him now, the old bastard. He must have been forty.

Towards the end of the week, I was assigned a new task – to bundle envelopes into stacks, using elastic bands, and then to stack the bundled stacks into larger stacks. While I was doing this, an old guy, about sixty, came up to me, and he elbowed me aside and said, 'watch this'. Over the years he had developed an ability to pick envelopes and slide elastic bands on to the envelopes with the speed of a conjuror; he did them all in two or three minutes. Somebody told me later that he was an office legend. He'd been there for ever. Two minutes it took him. It would have taken me half an hour.

The legend beamed at me. He was one of those quite nice old guys.

He said, 'Don't worry – when you've been here as long as I have, you'll be able to do this.'

But then I got another message to see Mr Webb.

'I'm going to have to let you go,' he said.

I'd been to the tea trolley again.

I'd forgotten to lock up my cheques again.

I've never had a proper job for very long. Sometimes I've made money, but I haven't saved a penny. Not many people do. We're not a saving society – we're a borrowing one. We save, on average, just 2 per cent of what we earn. It's the same across the Western world.

And why do we borrow so much? Because prices are always going up. And why are prices always going up? Because it's so easy to borrow money. Another reason we borrow is that we are full of hope. We borrow, hoping that something will turn up, believing something will turn up. Because, so far, it always has.

Maybe things will turn up for me.

Maybe . . .

And now, fatally, I've allowed hope to enter my mind. Whoever was guarding the checkpoints, on strict instructions to repel hope, was not doing their job. It's got in, and now it's rattling around, rattling around the channels of my mind, causing mayhem, like little spiky balls.

Little spiky balls of hope.

Hope can be the most terrible thing. When I used to go to boarding school, the worst moment was not, as you might think, the first night back after the summer holidays, but the last week of the holidays themselves.

Because you still had hope!

My holidays were a week longer, at each end, than most people's, so I had a week at the start of the summer when I was the only person on holiday, which was magical, and a week at the end, when everybody I knew had gone back to school, and I was again the only person on holiday. But that last week was terrible.

During that last week, I'd do stuff on my own; I'd go for walks, sit in the garden, but I'd be unsettled, feeling sick and anxious – I'd walk in the hills, or along the river, and come back home, my father already gone, my mother getting ready to go, suitcases half-packed, piles of folded, laundered stuff in the kitchen. Sometimes we'd go on an outing; we'd walk along the beach, which had seemed quite a different place even two weeks before, but now, with the September nip in the air, it was a quiet place, you were aware of the surf sucking and crashing, aware of the shingle crunching under your feet, and it would be slightly too cold to swim, and in any case I wouldn't have the heart for swimming. I remember walking along the beach in early September 1976, when I was sixteen, thinking that the next time I might even possibly be happy would be next summer, would be that magical week at the start of the holiday, and this made me think of the day, ten weeks earlier, when I'd cycled to the sea in the morning, and set up my rod on the pier, just me, sitting on the concrete struts, hanging my legs over the side, the sky clear, the sun glinting, the tide high, the water absolutely flat calm.

A sailing boat went past, and I was sure I recognised somebody on it, somebody from school, and the boy looked up when I shouted, and did not acknowledge me. I could see the whole bay. I still think of it as one of the happiest mornings of my life, seen as it was through the viewfinder of ten weeks later, when the memory of it pierced my defences as I walked along the beach, September's nip in the air, shingle crunching and slipping underfoot, the whole thing made sadder somehow because the holiday was not quite over; the holiday was still alive, breathing false hope.

And now I have false hope again, and this memory makes me think of last summer, when I was forty-six, when my little boy was eighteen months old, and my relationship with his mother was in the balance. We went on holiday for two weeks, driving down the coast, and we set off early, it was the day they roped in a gang of Muslims on a charge of 'plotting to blow up trans-atlantic aircraft', and I was incensed, the whole thing absolutely stank; it was when the Israelis were bombing Lebanon, and everybody was screaming at Blair to make a comment, and he wouldn't, he went into hiding, and then his own ministers started making a fuss about it, and one guy resigned, and two days later, what do you know, they'd rounded up a load of Muslims in the middle of the night, Muslims who were supposedly plotting to blow up transatlantic aircraft.

We set off at dawn, listening to the reports all the way down, with the sea on our left, and I kept saying I knew exactly what had happened – these were angry, disaffected Muslim guys they'd had their eye on for a while, and when the situation in Lebanon reached a crisis, to the extent that Blair was in a serious fix, they'd roped these guys in, saying they were plotting to blow up planes. This, I said, would turn public opinion, shut every-body up.

'This will never come to trial,' I kept saying.

I was on edge.

After two hours' driving, we stopped at a beach, and drank coffee out of a flask, and went for a walk along the beach with our little boy, watching the early joggers on the concrete path at the top of the sand, and I wonder if this will ever happen again, if we'll do this again, and I hope so, and the fact that my little boy is going on holiday tomorrow, without me, is something I don't want to think about.

Will we ever go on holiday again?

Will it happen?

Maybe it would be easier to know, for sure, that it *won't* happen, just as, thirty years ago, it was easier on the first night back in the dormitory, with everybody lined up along the beds for the housemaster's talk, jabbing each other in the kidneys; much easier to stand in the dormitory, being jabbed in the kidneys, than to walk along the beach and go back home to the half-packed suitcases and the last week of false hope.

The river bends to the left and the sun catches the river and the hope rattles around inside me, and I try to repel it, try to think of something else, such as dying societies, and my mind alights on the quotation at the start of Mel Gibson's film *Apocalypto* about the fact that civilisations are not killed but rather 'destroy themselves from within', and I remember the wise old one-armed guy in the film sitting by the campfire telling everybody about man's essential problem – he wants too much, and eventually the earth has no more to give. That's a pretty good summary of the human situation.

And it's not our elected representatives who give us that summary, by the way.

It's Mel Gibson.

Mel Gibson, the former 'sexiest man on earth', now wading through middle age, his face set in a scowl, his demons jumping out all over the place – Mel Gibson, with his drink-driving, his arrest, his 'are you a Jew?' yelled at the arresting officer. Deeply flawed Mel Gibson. This is the guy who tells us about the human situation, because democracy is ruined; we elect people who just want to keep the corporations happy; we elect people who want to keep the freight trains full of illusions.

Every society has a lifespan. First, it emerges from, or escapes from, the ruins of the society before. Then it establishes itself. Then it starts wanting too much, or wanting the wrong things.

Then it begins to decline, and one day it crumbles, and the next thing you know archaeologists are piecing it together, amazed at how dumb people were. This is what Mel Gibson is telling us.

Apocalypto! I'm thinking of the ritual executions, heads hurled down the steps, headless bodies bouncing down afterwards, a guy at the bottom catching the heads in some kind of net. Thinking about this helps me with my hope problem. I'm thinking about the hero darting through the jungle, the plants spooling past in full-screen panic mode, arrows zinging next to the guy's head, the hero flashing through the vegetation with the energy of sheer naked desperation, towards his threatened family, his wife and son, although wife is probably the wrong word, I'm thinking squaw, squaw might be the right word here. He's bound to die, you keep thinking, just like his friend died, the plumpish one who couldn't get his wife pregnant, poor guy, and who ended up on the deck with a spear in one side and out the other, gasping his last in the mud, biting the dust. One tribe sticking spears into another tribe, people having their hearts cut out, a terrible way to go, you'd think, but probably better than most, when you come down to it.

I turn and look across the river. In a morbid mood now, I think of death, and then of the deaths of people I have known, and my mind alights on the much-documented death of John Diamond, filed in my personal archives under Scary Deaths. John Diamond, who died surrounded by journalist friends, and wrote his thoughts on pieces of paper moments before he was finally put under, the last scripted thought being, as I remember reading, 'I'm tired of the pain and the waiting'.

I met Diamond twice, the second time being at a party before he'd been diagnosed with cancer of the throat and tongue. He had a lump on the side of his voice box, and we talked about the lump, and he said he'd seen a doctor about the lump, who had pronounced it safe, 'a cyst', and he told me he was greatly relieved. At the time, I was snorting coke and getting nosebleeds, and had some tenderness in my jaw and around my left ear; sometimes the area just behind my left ear became unbearably itchy, so much so that I would poke things into the ear itself, which was hopeless, which didn't stop the itching, if anything made it worse. At the time, I had raging hypochondria. So when I met Diamond, and had the talk about the lump, I went away relieved, my health fears abated; I carried on snorting coke, drinking heavily, smoking, overeating and drinking endless cups of black coffee; I carried on plundering my resources, eating into my seed capital, behaving as if it would last for ever, relieved that the cigar-smoking Diamond had a lump and the lump had been pronounced safe.

I never saw him again.

But I did read his cancer dispatches. They went on for years, and emanated a balance between acceptance and tragic hope, the hope that accompanied the purchase, close to death, of a gold Rolls-Royce. Oh, his searing memory, after his tongue had been removed, of an incident that occurred when he was 'fully glottal'; I can still remember reading those words, and then, afterwards, the posthumous report about the pain and the waiting.

So his doctor had been wrong. The lump was not safe; under attack, the cells of his throat and tongue had repaired themselves, over and over, until they had nothing left to give, until they crossed a crucial threshold and started to make mistakes, blundering on blindly past the point of no return.

Moving fast, with vegetation on my left, a series of trees set back from the river, I replace my John Diamond file in the Scary Deaths section of my brain, and set sail again, towards the mulch of facts, stored but not well organised, about dead societies.

Dead worlds. Like the Greenland Norse. For some reason I keep thinking about the Greenland Norse. They were the people who set sail from Norway, under the leadership of Erik the Red, the great chieftain, and settled in Greenland in the Middle Ages. This was after the Viking period, after the raping and pillaging – or, rather, after the classic era of raping and pillaging; you can't tell me it wasn't still going on in 1100.

Still, these people were religious. Not on a small scale, like the mud-hut Scots, my ancestors, with their scraggly sheep and a handful of oats in the sporran, to be washed down with water from the trout stream, the *burn*, hence Otterburn, Bannockburn. I'm thinking here of Rob Roy, *Braveheart*, of houses dug into the muddy sides of hills with turf on the roof, dour as hell. That was the Scots. But the *Norse* – the Norse did things on a bigger scale. Big churches, big feasts, big steaks. They loved their cows. They were cow people, cows and God, very aware of Satan. There was, I think, one huge church, a kind of centrepiece of Norse culture. They prayed, grew wheat and would have grown secondary crops to feed their cows, such as, I don't know, beets? Probably beets. I'd have to check. It might be there somewhere, in the weeds, in the mulch of my memory. Anyway, cows were the thing. Cows and churches.

I'm trying to picture them, the medieval Norse. They would not have worn horned helmets. They probably hated the sight of horned helmets. I imagine that horned helmets have a very long fashion cycle – once they're out, they'd be out for a long time. They must have gone berserk, too, the medieval Norse, but in a much more controlled way than they had, in the old days of raiding and spreadeagling. As far as I remember, they would get somebody, hold him down and cut his chest in half with an axe; I guess you had to be good at it, you'd be hopeless at first, the other guys would laugh at you afterwards, but you'd get better, and eventually you'd be able to split a chest with one crisp blow of the axe, and then someone would pull the heart out, while you stood there, in your horned helmet. In those days, they actually paid people to go berserk – the bear-serks. Going berserk was a job. And think what you'd have to do, as a bear-serk, when raping and spreadeagling was the *norm*. A very hard job to hold down, I imagine, having to go berserk in front of an audience of guys who had just spent time cleaving people in two and ripping their hearts out, a very tough audience. They must have got a lot of stage fright, the bear-serks.

But that all happened around – and I'm guessing here – AD 700. I guess Erik the Red's men would have worn iron helmets, not horned but with a nose guard. They'd have had rough smocks, all very puritanical, with some leatherwear – that's what I'm coming up with. They probably went berserk in a mild way, like those creepy rich guys who run around the woods naked, with body paint, people in charge of big corporations and guys who know Rumsfeld and Bush and Cheney.

Anyway, my point is that the Norse sailed to Greenland because life in Norway was becoming intolerable, which in turn was because of the invention of the plough, which made farming easier, which meant a spike in population, and suddenly everybody was scrabbling for resources. And the thing was, life had been getting better for quite a while because of the increased farming yields. Economic growth always leads to a crash.

So off they set, Erik at the helm, in their sailing boats, full, I suppose, of animal skins and cows and salt beef, and they landed in Greenland, which was colder and grimmer than Norway, but just about liveable, at a pinch. And what did they do when they landed? More or less the first thing was that they built a huge church, a replica of the one they'd left behind. That was the Norse. That set the tone. Then they prayed, raised cows, ploughed the soil, grew wheat, grew beets. And it was hard. The weather was not good. The soil was poor. But they could manage, just about. And they gritted their way through for about three centuries, with the cows and the praying, the beets and the wheat.

Meanwhile, who else was living in Greenland? The Inuit, of course. Ice fishermen and hunters of seals and porpoises, thirty words for snow and a hundred uses for a dead whale, nothing wasted, using the blubber as face cream and the bones to make harpoons, these guys had been in Greenland for ages. Igloos, for God's sake, and huskies pulling sledges along, which is the way to get around in the snow, and, incidentally, the real reason Amundsen beat Captain Scott to the South Pole, because he put his faith in dogs, unlike Scott, who put his in horses, which, if I remember, he kept eating along the way. Can that be right? Did Scott eat his horses? Now I'm not so sure. That would be like driving somewhere and eating your car, and then finding yourself stuck. It would be like Armstrong and Aldrin and the other one, I can never remember his name, landing on the moon and eating the lunar module, which of course is not true; it wouldn't be like that at all, and I don't even know if Scott ate his horses or not. I'll have to check my facts.

And for a moment I have a familiar pinprick of regret: if only I could go back in time and start my education now, and do it properly this time around, spend more time in the library, rather than smoking dope and trying to run a mobile disco . . .

I blew it!

Shit, shit, *shit*.

Now I'm lost, my boat bobbing in the current; I grab the sail and wrench it around, back to the Norse. What I was going to say was this: something terrible happened to them. For a while their winters, already very punitive, got worse. Their topsoil eroded. The wheat crop failed several years in a row. They had to eat the food they grew for their cattle, so their cattle starved.

Then they ate all their cattle, and then the horses, and then the dogs, and then they died themselves, leaving nothing but the big church.

And never once did they learn to fish!

We know this because archaeologists have dug up their remains; there are bones from cattle and horses, and butchered dog bones, but no fish bones. And yet a few miles away, in Inuit territory, they were feasting on fish. Remember, this is before these places were fished out. This was when you could chuck your bait in the water and haul out tons of mackerel, and cod and so forth. But the Norse didn't eat fish, because they defined themselves as people who simply didn't do that. It was below them. The whole point of life was to be a cow-and-God person, a non-fish-eater, not like those stinky old Eskimos with their thirty words for snow.

We, the Norse, have only one word for snow, and that's 'snow'.

Got it?

And we are cow-eaters!

That was the mindset. But why? In his book *Collapse*, the anthropologist Jared Diamond answers the question. He says that the Norse were more interested in *being the Norse* than in survival itself: right up until the very end, the big thing for them was their identity as God-fearing cow people, as people who didn't eat fish. It really mattered to them.

I'm standing on the bank, looking at the bridge across the river. Societies destroy themselves. That's Jared Diamond's point. That was the old man's point in *Apocalypto*. Societies destroy themselves, but the people in them don't know they're doing it. They just get stuck in a rut, doing the things they've always done, making them into rituals, religions, and when the religions stop working they carry on with them anyway, thinking something will turn up, because it has always turned up.

Because they're full of hope.

One of the worst examples, although not the very worst example, is the Easter Islanders. Easter Island is a tiny speck in the Pacific, somewhere between New Zealand and Chile. A Dutch explorer – I forget his name, something like Van Meergen or Amstelveen, something with an 'ee' sound in it – found the island a couple of hundred years ago, on Easter Day, hence the name. When I say Amstelveen, or whatever he was called, found the island, I mean him and about a hundred other people, a ship full of people, or more likely several ships.

It's quite confusing, I think, when you go to school and learn that, say, Captain Cook discovered Australia, or that Stanley found Livingstone in the jungle. You imagine Stanley and Livingstone were each on their own, two white guys wandering towards each other through a forest, although you don't imagine an ordinary forest, but a much darker, more tangled forest, with big, fat, wet leaves, and lots of snakes and monkeys. In fact, as a kid, I imagined Africa to be *all* jungle, whereas, when I went there, and flew across the southern part of it in a tiny plane, it seemed to be more or less all scrubland and rocks. Anyway, I imagined Livingstone and Stanley, having each woken up in a tent, having both gone on a walk, a 'morning constitutional' through the jungle, to have bumped into each other in a clearing, Stanley saying his famous words – 'Dr Livingstone, I presume?' – knowing they would pass into history as a masterpiece of wit. What happened next? Maybe the two men became friends or something; nobody told me. What I'm getting at, though, is that it wouldn't just have been Stanley and Livingstone; it was those two, *and their entourages*, lots of white guys, perhaps even hundreds, who had come to Africa with their guns and bibles, not on a camping trip, but because their own societies were beginning to run out of natural resources, and they were out there looking for more.

*   *   *

I went to Africa once. Actually, I went twice, if you count a trip to Morocco when I was a student. The Moroccan trip was with a guy called Robin. I was twenty-three and he was twenty-one. I envied the fact that he was slightly more than a year younger than me. I really did. He was studying physics, and wanted to take his studies on to CERN, the physics lab in Switzerland where they smash atoms together to see what happens to the tiny particles inside the atoms. Robin was fascinated by atoms. They clump together, making objects and creatures. No one really knows why. Then they fall apart.

I went to southern Africa to write a story on the two remaining kings of African countries who had been to English boarding schools, as I had, and I sat down and had tea with this particular king, in his palace. Outside the palace, a crowd of disaffected people had gathered. I wondered if the King had thought about going out on the balcony and addressing the crowd. But he didn't think it would do any good. The tea – the pot and the cups and the biscuits – made me think of English people coming to Africa to see what they could find, because they were running out of stuff at home on account of the Industrial Revolution, democracy and so forth; the teapot made me think of all those Victorians scouring the globe to get more stuff, and getting it, and leaving a few things behind, such as teapots.

Just like the Easter Islanders, setting off in their boats towards this tiny island in the middle of nowhere, presumably because their own societies, in Tonga and Fiji, had no room for them. What's the definition of an overcrowded society? A successful one. Tonga and Fiji must have got too successful, with their farming methods, their ploughs. They must have had a population boom. So some of them set off in their boats, looking for somewhere to live, and they found it, this island the size of a

73

small city, in the middle of the Pacific, one of the remotest places on earth. And how did they know it was there? Because of the flight patterns of seabirds. Experienced prehistoric sailors could map the sea many miles ahead of them by watching birds in the sky; there was a complicated language of birdwatching – an albatross going this way, at this speed, followed by a small group of terns doing this or that. They knew which direction to paddle in.

And Amstelveen – that's not his name but you know who I mean – Amstelveen and his boatloads of Dutch sailors were absolutely shocked when they landed in this place. Because it was practically deserted, and full of these enormous statues, hundreds of enormous statues across the island. And when archaeologists worked out what had happened, over the next couple of hundred years, they were shocked, too.

The big mystery was: how had the people who lived on the island transported the statues? And where had the people all gone? What they found was that the island had been covered with enormous palm trees. The Easter Islanders had made roads out of wood, and they'd made ropes out of tree bark. They'd carved the statues, huge things as high as buildings, and they'd hauled the statues across the island, hundreds of guys at a time.

They'd also used the trees as raw material for canoes, and they'd grown crops, and hunted their protein out of the sea. But they kept chopping down the trees. The place was divided into several kingdoms, and each kingdom wanted to have the biggest statues. So they'd fish, and farm, and carve, and chop down trees, always needing more wooden roads, more manpower, bigger statues, and you've probably seen them, the statues, they look semi-creepy, looming over the island, with blank stares on their faces and these enormous hat things on their heads.

And then the Easter Islanders ran out of trees. That's what Jared Diamond says. Can you imagine that? They chopped them

74

all down, the need for statues foremost in their minds, although they must have had the black shadows, the feelings of self-loathing and guilt that take people over as societies die, when a small but significant number of people hate themselves so much they turn into perverts and serial killers; there must, I suppose, have been an Easter Island version of Ted Bundy. He'd have travelled along with the statue-raising party, then he'd have sneaked off into the next little kingdom, with his arm in a sling like Bundy did, getting young women to help him out, and then boom. Bundy used chloroform, didn't he? I don't suppose they had chloroform on Easter Island, but then you'd be amazed what they did have in those places; we think we're so great, don't we, with our chloroform and Prozac, but they had natural versions of things, didn't they? So it's possible.

And the big question is: when the Easter Islander chopped down the last tree, *what was he thinking?*

My headache is settling into a flat, dull pain, and the fever is battling it out with the light cavalry of my endorphins. It's too early to tell who will win that battle. The coffee effect is slipping, too – I'm still edgy, but the initial jangle has died down. Standing here, looking at the brown water below, I can feel the first hints of the bone-tiredness that will take me over as the morning wears on.

The sky is streaky.

There's a blanket of grey behind me, blowing towards the town.

A man is in the crown of one of the riverside trees, lopping branches with a chainsaw, and there's another guy setting up a wood-chipper, which makes me think of a book I found in a second-hand shop, *The Wood-Chipper Killer*, about an air hostess who didn't turn up for work one day at, I think, La Guardia airport in New York, but because she was an air hostess, and flew all over the world, nobody raised the alarm, allowing her husband the crucial day or two to dispose of her body – he'd killed her – and almost get away with it. What he did was this: he kept telling people she was staying with her mother, and he kept telling her mother she was on a long-haul flight, meanwhile renting a wood-chipper and feeding her body into it by the side of a stream, thinking this would totally get rid of the body, rather than just fill this little stream with chopped-up bits of her, and now he's in jail, the sick individual. Richard something.

That was another thing about me and the mother of my little boy; she liked crime fiction, and I like crime fiction, too, but I prefer true crime. Like, once I came home with this book, *Murder in Greenwich*, by Mark Fuhrman. I was bowled over. It was a reopening of the Martha Moxley case, in which a rich girl had been beaten to death, and the author was, of all people, Detective Fuhrman, the cop who'd caused the N-word furore in the O. J. Simpson case. It was like the World Series of true crime. I was pretty enthusiastic about it. I also got the DVD version, and we watched that.

Another thing is that, when it comes to fiction, the mother of my little boy likes heroic characters, whereas what I like is anti-heroes. I don't just like my narrators to be flawed; I like them to be out-and-out bums and failures.

Her big hero of all time, by the way, is Horatio Nelson. He was intelligent, decisive, unsentimental. He was more or less the same, character-wise, as Tom Hanks in *Saving Private Ryan*. We've stood on the spot where he died, and we've been to see the clothes he died in, the jacket with the tiny hole in the shoulder where the fatal musket ball went in, and the bloodstained stockings – some of the blood having come from another guy who died at Nelson's feet and bled into his boots. That's what it was like, at Trafalgar – lead balls pinging through the air, not constantly, but sporadically, so that, on deck, you'd have one within a yard or two every minute or so. And then there were cannonballs, of course, and the deadly splinters from the ship's hull, oak splinters the size of Kitchen Devils coming at you at, say, 300 mph. Trafalgar in 1805 was the last big wooden battle; by then, most of the trees in Europe had been chopped down and everybody was waiting for the next big thing, which was sinking mineshafts to get coal, coal being yesterday's trees, rotted down and calcified into rocks, and so a better source of energy. With coal, you can have furnaces, which means you can make iron and steel on a large scale, leading to iron-clad ships, and therefore the need to invent missiles that explode on impact, because otherwise how are you going to sink an iron-clad ship?

Recently, over the last couple of years, I've had some strange psychological symptoms. During this time, on a typical day, I would wake up, have breakfast, say goodbye to my little boy and his mother, walk to my office, sit down at my desk, and then – nothing.

My mind hasn't been working properly. My thoughts are there, darting around, but they're much more elusive than usual.

This has happened every day for maybe five hundred days. But I should not complain; it's natural. It happens to people when they get to the point in life when nature has finished with them – or, rather, when nature would have finished with them in the Stone Age. When nature's finished with you, you start to fall apart.

So for the last five hundred days I've been walking into my office, and trying to get my thoughts going, and failing. Am I like the guy in *The Shining*? He was a writer, he was middle-aged, he had a wife and child, he began to lose his mind; he pretended, on the surface, that everything was fine, he deliberately got a winter job in a place that would be snowbound, to give him the best possible chance to write. Then he found that he couldn't write, and yet still sat there, writing the same line over and over. It's a great scene, isn't it, when the wife finds the stack of pages he's written, she's already begun to suspect he's gone crazy, and she sees the first page, and he's written the same line, over and over: 'All work and no play makes Jack a dull boy.' And then she looks at the second page, and it's the same. And then – this is the crucial moment – she looks in the middle of the stack, and for the first time she knows for certain that her husband is cracked, that he's mad. The sort of person that might go on some kind of mad rampage.

I walk back on the other side of the river, past the warehouses, through the shopping precinct with its cheap shoes and cheap medicines and the two health stores which, I am sure, are really sweet shops in disguise, but how do I know, I'm paranoid, I am cracking up, I am a part-time conspiracy theorist, I obsess about the explosions on 9/11 that supposedly preceded the planes flying into the towers, I've watched the DVDs, heard the soundtrack, and I try not to think about this, but sometimes I can't help it.

I keep thinking, 'It's just like JFK!'

I once read this book about the JFK assassination by the young doctor on call at the Dallas hospital on the fateful day, and he was in the room with Kennedy's body, working on the shattered head, the splattered brains, and he realised that there were some men in the room, they were wearing dark suits and ties – *where did they come from?* – and then, when the coroner came to pick up the body, they wouldn't let him have it, they threatened him with guns.

Dark suits and ties, they were wearing.

I remember taping a JFK documentary, a serious conspiracy job with computer animations, with graphic versions of Kennedy being rotated around, so you could see the trajectory of bullets and so on. I watched it with the mother of my little boy, and she was not impressed, not impressed at all, and another time I remember explaining exactly how the O. J. Simpson case worked, talking about Simpson's lawyer Barry Scheck, how he refuted the DNA evidence with his brilliant, nerdy, logic-chopping speech about how it doesn't matter if there's a one in however many billion chance the blood in question was not Simpson's, if you have even a small suspicion that someone planted it.

That was just before I ran out of money. If I'd had a psychiatric assessment at that point, he or she should have checked my O. J. Simpson levels, and also my residual levels of JFK assassination, RFK assassination, Chappaquiddick, Ted Bundy, and the Hanratty case. The psychiatrist would have noticed creeping 9/11 symptoms, too. That's what happens when I start to crack up – I get all conspiracy-minded.

Past the sweet shops disguised as health food stores, and past the café. Then I slip back into the newsagent's, and look at news-papers, catching the headlines about the missing child, the falling market, the death of sport and the end of love, and I buy another newspaper, just one more, and then I walk back along the road to my office. When I walk up the stairs, my heart rattles in my chest, and when I get back inside I go straight to my bed and lie down. It's five minutes before I get up and go to the bathroom.

Back when I was shitting blood, a few years ago, I had a weird experience. I was drinking heavily. I was full of pain. I had pain in my neck, my head and my abdomen, and pain around the lump in my leg. One day I read an article about the actor Mark Ruffalo. He dreamed he had a brain tumour, and went to the doctor; and it turned out, not what you'd expect, not that he didn't have a brain tumour, but that he did have a brain tumour, in one of the places that scares me most – behind the ear. It turned out to be benign.

This, I was thinking, is what happened to my friend Mark. As middle age approached, he became depressed, and he couldn't work, and the depression got deeper, and just at the point where it looked like it might have settled, he began to lose the hearing in his right ear.

Was this creeping middle age?

Or something worse?

Then the hearing went completely, and it turned out he had a benign tumour behind the ear, like Mark Ruffalo, although, unlike Mark Ruffalo, my friend Mark had an operation to remove the tumour that was only semi-successful, leaving him paralysed down one side of his face, and then he found out that the tumour had grown back, had come back, that he'd have to have another operation, that his face might get even worse, and this was when he decided to go to Australia. He wanted to go to Australia, travel around Australia, before his operation.

I said goodbye to Mark. I remember the exact moment, standing on a street, saying, 'I'll see you to the station.'

Him saying, 'No, it's all right, it's only up the road.'

'No, but I'll see you to the station.'

'No, honestly.'

'Well, okay then.'

And I remember him walking up the road a bit, and crossing the road, and then he was out of sight, and he sent me a postcard from Australia, and then his sister called, telling me he'd been knocked down by a bus at night, on a quiet road, and telling me about his body, how his body would have to be air-freighted, although I don't think she used the word 'body' or the expression 'air-freighted', but that's what she was talking about, the body in the hold of the plane, the cold hold. Do they refrigerate them? Surely it's freezing in there anyway, above 35,000 feet, at the edge of the atmosphere, in the hold with the suitcases?

After you've had these thoughts, you sometimes get on a plane and wonder if there's a dead person in there next to your suitcases.

The funeral was one of those quiet, very sad ones, not at all like the funeral of a grandparent, and I stood up in the church and read Shakespeare's sonnet about the passing of time, number 55, and when I came to the part that goes 'You shall shine more bright in the contents/Than unswept stone, besmear'd with sluttish time', I couldn't say the word 'sluttish', because the context was wrong. I could see the word, but couldn't say it – the funeral was so sad – so I said 'besmear'd with *troubled* time', and I think nobody noticed, even though Shakespeare's point had not been that time was troubled, not that we had to sympathise with time, but that time was sluttish, time seduced you into thinking things were okay when they weren't okay, precisely because people die and bindweed grows over their gravestones, and even their *gravestones* die, that's what he was saying, that was his point. Not that time had anything to worry about – time was the villain of the piece. As I say, I think nobody noticed, and afterwards we went back and had some tea and sandwiches at Mark's mother's house, where everybody was putting a brave face on things.

So the Mark Ruffalo article made me think. I was sitting in this particular Starbucks; it was right opposite the only newsagents I knew where I could get the American version of *Esquire* magazine, which I was reading because of a series by a guy who had bowel cancer. Remember, I was shitting blood, and I didn't want to go to the doctor, because I didn't want to find out that I was dying – I would rather die, I realised, than *find out* I was dying, so I didn't go to the doctor, thinking I'd just ride it out, it might be a temporary thing. And there's no way you can find proper statistics about these things *anywhere*, just like with moles. You can find out that most abnormal mole growth is benign, most dark moles are benign, most moles with ragged edges are benign, and you can find out that sometimes shitting blood is close to fine – or it might not be cancer, anyway. But nowhere does anybody give you a straight percentage, or even a ballpark figure. You don't know if 99 per cent of ragged, mottled moles are benign, or if 99 per cent are cancerous. You don't know if most people who shit blood are dying, or if most are not. The advice is never: weigh up the odds, then decide. The advice is always: if you're worried about a mole, or if you're shitting blood, *see a doctor*.

But I didn't want to see a doctor.

I didn't want to find out I was dying.

I would rather die, I thought, than find out I was dying.

Dying contains hope, doesn't it?

But death does not; death is like the first night back at boarding school, standing by the bed, being poked in the kidneys.

Dying is like the last week of the holiday.

Suitcases lying open, things being laundered and folded. The walk on the beach. The nip in the air.

So, of course, I was interested in this bowel cancer series. It was superbly well written – the story, brilliantly told, of the guy's symptoms, vague at first, just listlessness, slight bowel dysfunction, and something like a pinching pain in his abdomen. Then the doc told him the news – he had the big C. Terrible. But did I? I certainly had the pinching pains, the bowel dysfunction, the listlessness. I had just begun to notice that my mind was growing weeds. My thoughts were there, just like before, but more elusive than usual; I would launch my little boat, and it would get tangled in the weeds.

Every month, as the publication date came around again, I would walk to the newsagents and buy the magazine and sit in the Starbucks and read about this guy and his bowel cancer.

I had a ride-out time of five years.

Five years before this, when I was on a day trip with my ex and her mother, and my ex's dog, I remember shitting blood. We had caught the train from London to Cambridge, and everything that might have gone wrong went wrong; the trip was a disaster. I panicked, or choked, and couldn't think straight, and then there was the incident in the lavatory, with the blood, and the women ended up walking off together, leaving me with the dog, the damn dog.

And every year after that, I kept thinking: this has been going on for a year, and I'm not dead, and then, eventually, this has been going on for five years, and I'm not dead, so I must be riding it out. Just like in 1985, when I was terrified I'd caught HIV, but did not want to think about it, focusing instead on the fact that Aids, or 'full-blown Aids', as we said then, almost always appears within a decade of infection, so as 1995 rolled into view, I began to anticipate a small celebration. And now I'm hardly worried about Aids at all – a dangerous situation, no doubt.

Anyway, there I was, in Starbucks, reading about the guy and his bowel cancer. I followed the progress of his treatment. He went under the knife. He had a section of his bowel removed. He was forced to use a colostomy bag. He had to shit through what he called a 'stoma' – a hole in his side. There were pictures of him looking pale and thin. This was all happening in America. Then one day I read something that chilled me. He said something about walking down a street in London called England's Lane.

That was the name of the street where I was sitting, in the Starbucks.

The Starbucks was in England's Lane.

Spooky.

Another day, I was sitting in the Starbucks, by the window, feeling a little off colour, looking out of the window.

And this guy looked at me through the window.

It was him!

It was the bowel cancer guy.

His head inches from mine.

And we smiled at each other, and he came in, got a coffee. A week later, I was going to the newsagent *to get my copy of* Esquire, in other words to get my copy of *Esquire to see how this guy's treatment was progressing*, and, at that very moment, he passed me on the street, himself heading into the Starbucks.

We looked at each other.

He said, 'How are you?'

I said, 'Fine.'

I never saw him after that.

On the wall in the bathroom, at grab height if I'm sitting down, is a plywood rack, with three books and a crumpled bushel of once-glossy magazines which now have a frilly bathroom look. The books. These are the books that have migrated here, at certain intense moments, and stayed: *Down and Dirty Pictures*, a book about independent cinema in the 1990s; *The Kenneth Williams Diaries*; *Nelson: A Medical Casebook*. I open Kenneth Williams, and, with my right thumb, flick through the second half of the book, the half that describes Williams' intensifying gloom and stomach and bowel dysfunction. I catch the odd word: 'waste', 'unhealthy', 'toupee', 'gastroscopy'. When he was my age exactly, he had a 'sigmoidoscopy', a tube inserted into the rectum. 'The entire experience,' he wrote, 'was utterly delightful.' The day before he died, fifteen years later, he watched the news ('the dreary saga of murder & mayhem') and wrote his last words: 'Oh – what's the bloody point?'

Everything is fine, more or less. No blood. I think it was the drinking. I feel more optimistic and relaxed.

I might get through this.

And maybe the big romance of my life, whether it's with the mother of my little boy or somebody else, lies in the future.

Romance!

But I'm forty-seven!

Then, for a piercing moment, the force of this fact hits home. I'm forty-seven! Not thirty-seven! The other day, I woke up, feeling terrible, and I thought, My God, I'm forty-seven, and then I thought, calm down, that's not true – I'm thirty-seven. And I calmed down for a couple of seconds. Thirty-seven was still pretty bad, I thought. But forty-seven! Where had that idea come from? And then I fully woke up. I *was* forty-seven.

It's true. I am.

And my parents will die!

Maybe not for a while.

But that's what I *used* to say. I can't hide from this for much longer. They *will* die. Damn! My mother has recently had an operation for malignant melanoma, a cancerous mole, and the operation was a success – the doc predicted a total cure, and the subsequent check-up was fine. On top of that, five years ago she had temporal arteritis, a condition in which the arteries in the temples, close to the eyes, become inflamed, and you get blinding headaches; she took a course of steroids, never a good thing to do, but it seemed to work. It might and might not come back. Probably not, they say. It's an auto-immune disease, in which the immune system, the gunners in the turrets overlooking the beach, make mistakes and panic and start shooting each other, a sudden blast of friendly fire. And when the gunners have shot

85

each other once, there is a chance they'll go crazy and start shooting at each other again. But they might not. She is seventy-five tomorrow.

My father, five years older, has an irregular heartbeat, something he's had ever since he contracted rheumatic fever as a child. This means he must take warfarin, a blood-thinning drug, famously used as a rat poison. Again, not a good thing to do. Recently he cut his leg, and the cut hasn't healed, and it's become infected, and the infection won't go away, and the fact that he takes warfarin means he can't take the antibiotics he should take, but must take other, less good, ones. He smoked until he was around fifty, and still drinks, but has no cancer, and never has had; he also has most of his hair and very low readings of LDL cholesterol – very few spiky balls, even though his blood pressure is higher than it should be.

My parents are fine, considering.

But they will die. Secretly, I fear that they will both die at the age of eighty-three, or thereabouts – meaning that he will die in three years, her in eight. But the average age of my grandparents at death was eighty-seven, and they grew up in worse conditions, ate worse food, and the men both smoked three-quarters of a million cigarettes, far more than my father, who smoked twenty a day until he was thirty, followed by a pipe until the age of fifty.

Fifty?

I'm nearly fifty myself.

In the kitchen I get everything ready for my anti-ageing porridge, and, while I'm doing this, I look out of the window at the hill I'll be climbing later, when I go to pick up my little boy for the last time before the start of the holiday, and something funny happens to my heart; it flaps away, the bird in the cage, and then stops, the pause in blood flow making my head go funny for a second, or maybe it's my imagination. But I don't think so. When this happens, which isn't every day, but perhaps every other day, I imagine my heart gulping my blood, like a hungry mouth, like Bobby with his can of beer, the ventricles gulping, slurping, then catching on a thick bit, choking on a clot, and flapping, breaking the clot up, and then grinding back into rhythm.

The porridge is as follows:

Some flaked quinoa, a grain with a low glycaemic index, a low 'GI', which means it doesn't break down into glucose in the blood too quickly, and so does not put a strain on the pancreas gland.

Some oats, but not many.

Some rye flakes.

Ground almonds.

Goji berries – like raisins, but with more vitamins.

Raisins.

A handful of seeds – pumpkin seeds, linseeds, sesame seeds, sunflower seeds.

I eat the porridge carefully, trying not to gulp or inhale it, and afterwards I sit down on my sofa and try to organise my work. I've made myself a cup of herbal tea. I'll check on the panicking and choking article. Then I'll try to do some writing. The prospect of this raises my blood pressure slightly and makes the porridge sit in my stomach like a bowlful of pebbles. Something has happened to my stomach recently; if I eat even slightly too much, it feels tender and sickish, which might be a good thing. I'm certainly losing weight – not, I hope 'sudden, un-explained weight loss', but gradual, seemly weight loss. I'm losing weight, down from a high point of 240 lb, when I used to overeat, to 196 lb now, but I'm still flabby, still not great. But this stomach thing. It's probably nothing. A friend's father had a bad stomach. He was about sixty. He ignored it for a while, and then it flared up again, and he got it checked out. They wouldn't let him leave the hospital. He was terminal, a couple of weeks from the end. He had cancer, and it had spread. So he stayed in bed. People visited.

I sip my herbal tea.

I sip my herbal tea as the spiky balls bounce off the sides of my arteries, whump-whump, whump-whump, whumpity-whumpity . . . whump-whump.

Some of the spiky balls are abrading the walls of my arteries. I think I can feel it happening.

My brain is not totally shot. It works, sometimes very clearly, for a small part of each day. Now is not that small part. Often, my thoughts make sense at the moment I have them; it's just getting them down that's the problem, getting them down – or, rather, up, getting them up on a screen.

I sit at the computer. Now I can't concentrate. In front of the screen I have stage fright. I choke.

I try to kick-start my mind into having some ideas. I ask myself questions.

Why do things end?

Things end because they fail. They fail because they change. They change because of time.

People die because of time.

And then their gravestones die because of time.

But this is not true. Einstein taught us that time doesn't make things change. He said that change made us believe in time. So time, in fact, is an illusion brought about by our perceptions of the way things have changed. You look at a coffin in a grave, and think – it's *time* that did that, time that put that guy in the coffin, time that made mistakes behind my friend Mark's ear, which made his face go funny, which made him want to run away to Australia, where he got run over by the bus. Time is the culprit, as well as being the slut, making us feel that things are okay, that we have more of everything, when we don't.

But Einstein showed us that time doesn't exist. Change exists, but not time. Observing change, we think we see time. But time is not real; only change is real.

We die because we change. And when we change, bits of us make mistakes. And mistakes beget mistakes. The cod dies because it gets too big. For the cod, getting too big is a mistake. The economy is in trouble because it's getting too big. For the economy, getting too big is a mistake.

And why do cod, and economies, make mistakes?

Well, as Tom Kirkland says, living things make mistakes because, after a while, *there is no reason for them not to.*

There is only a reason for them not to before they have passed on their genes.

After that, there is no reason for them not to make mistakes.

Economies make mistakes because they are all Ponzi schemes.

To work, they must grow.

The economy is, essentially, a cod.

A cod that's got too big.

And now my brain hurts. It's working, but in a haphazard fashion. To make it work properly, I need to go on a brisk walk. But when I'm on a brisk walk, I'm not sitting at my computer, so I can't get my thoughts down.

I mean up.

I've tried everything. I've tried taking notes on scraps of paper, and I've tried carrying a Dictaphone with me, and speaking into the Dictaphone when I have an idea. When I do this, people look at me and think I'm eccentric.

Eccentricity is lovable in the young.

But less lovable when you get older.

＊　　＊　　＊

89

My emails:

'Megadik stimulates cell growth within the corpus cavernosa itself . . . making the penis larger and the erection more intense.'

An editor writes, asking if I would be interested in writing about the subject of 'binge fucking'.

I'll get back to him.

And then there's the possibility of doing a few minutes' research on 'raw, meaty bones' – because there is, I think, a worthwhile story in there, and there's an Australian vet who has taken up the cause, and you can watch online TV clips of the guy promoting the concept of raw meaty bones. He seems like a nice guy. I could email him; once I got started, the story would take off. That's how I used to work, by plunging in regardless, hoping the momentum would build up by itself, and by and large this was a good method, come to think of it that's how I lived my life in every sense until the age of forty or so, plunging in and hoping.

Plunging and hoping: I remember meeting a guy when I was a teenager who said he knew where he could find a ladder, and he thought if he put the ladder up to the window of this Austrian chambermaid (she worked at a hotel) he thought that if he put a ladder up to her window – this was at night – she would kiss us. So I found myself hanging from the underside of the ladder while this guy kissed the girl through the window; she wouldn't let him in or anything, and when it was my turn we swapped over, very dangerous because we were drunk, and I kissed the Austrian girl for about five minutes, not bad at all, and then, when we swapped over a second time, I slipped and fell off the ladder, but by some amazing fluke landed on a plastic bin, my bottom inverting the lid of the bin, so although I was stuck in the bin I was totally unharmed. And that's how I used to do things – by plunging in and hoping to build momentum, and not caring if things did not work out.

But something, I don't know what, stops me from emailing the Australian vet, or even rewatching the television clips, which I've done a few times already.

For a moment I think of the Australian guy's cheerful face. I could get involved with the Australian guy.

Raw meaty bones!

. . . but I let myself become distracted by magazines, and flip though their slippery pages, looking at car ads.

The diarist Alan Clark said that the best cars were made around 1905, some of which work as well now as they did then, and that since then it's all been downhill – now, if cars were built to last, all the manufacturers would go out of business. People want to change their cars every couple of years anyway. This makes me think of an argument I had with a woman I lived with in 1994; she wanted to decorate our flat with all these things, to make it look nice, and I said what you really mean is that these things will make it look very 1994. We think they look nice now, I said, but in ten years we'll be able to see that, actually, they were very 1994. But she wouldn't accept this, would not accept this in any way, and I knew, right then, that we were wrong for each other, even though I did nothing about it, I let years slip through my fingers in this relationship.

Years.

I thought I had an endless supply of years.

And now I go to my bookshelf and flip through the last volume of Alan Clark's diaries, the posthumous one, looking for the bit about the 1905 car, the Rolls-Royce he drove around for fun just before he died, rather like John Diamond did, but I can't find the passage about the car, so I sit and read the bits about his illness and death. He keeps feeling strangely tired, inexplicably shattered, 'chesty', feverish, 'lassitudinous'. He worries about an infected patch on his leg. He has colds. Sometimes he feels 'sub-prostatic'. He describes 'a fairly constant strain always in the groin after peeing'. He often feels 'strange', and 'odd', and not quite himself. He has trouble sleeping. He sweats in the night, which I don't, and then he describes himself as 'very sleepy and slow and uninterested'.

He gets depressed.

He suffers from headaches on waking.

'I feel viral,' he says, towards the end.

He has things checked out. His liver is fine. His kidneys are fine. His pancreas is fine. His heart is fine.

He begins to think it's all in the mind.

Then he collapses; he has a 'massive tumour' in the brain.

'My brain seems to operate on two halves,' he writes. 'The second one is muddled and potentially obsessional. I have been quite wary of it for some weeks. It seems to subsist on creating bogus problems and then attaching spurious solutions to them.'

I put the book back, not wanting to get to the end, and pick up a magazine, and walk back into my bedroom, and fall on my bed, slightly awkwardly, and arrange a cushion behind me. There is a new tingling in my neck and shoulder area. I get up.

It feels like getting up in the middle of the night. In the bathroom I look at my face – not bad from a distance, but close up it's a battlefield of falling flesh and seeping pores. There's a tiny nodule at the tip of my nose, just like the nodule I had on my chin a few years ago. You have to watch these nodules – I once slightly knew a guy who had a nodule on his chin that grew and grew, until it became the focus of his face, like a new feature. And I knew this other guy who had a nodule on the side of his head, next to one of his eyes, and one day the end of it had erupted, and was dark and bloody, giving the impression he had three eyes. The longer you leave a nodule, the harder it is to deal with. You have to catch them early. I had my chin nodule cored out with an implement called a curette. I lay down, and the doc injected my chin four times, four lancing pains, and then he did his work with the curette, which he described as being like a tiny, razor-sharp ice-cream scoop. He also removed some cysts from my head, and one from my back. The cysts were trivial, imperfections of my ageing skin. The nodule was sent to the lab, where they put it under a microscope.

It wasn't cancerous.

Now I'm back on my bed. My sense of time has drifted. I'm tired. I'm always tired, and that's worrying. Constant tiredness is not always the result of serious illness, but a diagnosis of cancer or heart disease is almost always prefigured by constant tiredness – TAT syndrome, when you are 'tired all the time'. A woman I know was recently diagnosed with cancer; she suspected it a long time before the doctors could find anything, because she was a runner, and one day, her timing was off, and the next day, her recovery was slower than normal. She could run ten miles, but she knew something was wrong because she was slightly more tired than usual.

If pushed, I guess I could run maybe half a mile.

Flipping through my magazine, the supplement of a liberal, green-leaning newspaper, I look at the ads.

Car, anti-ageing product, electricity, mobile phones, car, cat food, credit card, alcohol, alcohol, car, bank, laptop, juice drink, eco-furniture, furniture, window blinds, kitchen units, olive oil, cookery books, beer, furniture, furniture, paint rollers, sofas, travel bags, bicycles, furniture, car.

* * *

A celebrity questionnaire asks: **When were you happiest?**

That's easy. Three days after my little boy was born, when the doctor told me he'd survive. 'He vill survive,' he said. I still remember the moment. There had been doubt. Oh, the doubt! But then: 'He vill survive.' I cried. I said, 'I'm sorry – I'm crying.' As if the doctor couldn't see I was crying. As if he didn't see this sort of thing every day. I cried. Then I stopped crying. I didn't want to leave the boy. He didn't have a name yet. He was in an oxygen box. But I had to leave him. I had to go back to the hotel. I was staying in a hotel, in a seaside resort, but it was off-season, so it was mostly empty. When I went to breakfast in the mornings, there was one other man; he was in his eighties. He told me he came to this hotel every year because it was where he'd stayed with his wife on their honeymoon, and they'd stayed there afterwards, too, in the 1950s and 1960s. He did not say where his wife was now. He said he liked going on the same walks he'd been on with her.

He'd been in the RAF during the war. He'd been in a squadron of English and Polish airmen. He loved the Poles, this guy. You could tell.

Every day, we were the only ones at breakfast. It was bright, sparkly weather. It looked like summer but felt cold. My son's life was in the balance for three days. I did not mention this to the old man. On the third day, the doctor said, 'He vill survive.' Then I cried. Then I said I was sorry. I said, 'I'm crying.' As if the doctor couldn't see. As if he didn't see this sort of thing every day. I didn't want to leave the boy. I went to see his mother, my partner, in the ward, and told her the news, and did not cry, but cried later, briefly, and then went back to the hotel. It was the very end of a wedding reception. There was a middle-aged woman going mad in the hotel bar. The barman was trying to call the police. But I intervened. That's when I was happiest.

What is your greatest fear?

That my son goes missing. That my son dies.

Property aside, what is the most expensive thing you've ever bought?

Again easy. I was thirty-three, and I drank, and I occasionally snorted cocaine, and I quite liked it, but then, one day, in March 1994, I bought a gram, costing me £70, and I snorted it, and something changed; it was as if I suddenly understood something I hadn't understood before, like looking at that picture which is a vase, which then becomes two faces, and you can never see it as just a vase any more. I bought that gram of coke, and something changed. I was thirty-three, and I didn't want to face up to the fact. A decade later I felt more like fifty-three. I was ruined in several senses. So I'd have to say that gram of coke was the most expensive thing I've ever bought. The man who sold it to me, Derek, went to prison, and quite right, too.

He once told me something that made me come of age. It was a Monday evening. The day before, I'd read an article in a Sunday newspaper. The article was about drinking clubs, and the writer had rated each club according to several categories – the food, the atmosphere, and so on – and one of the categories was whether you could buy cocaine at the club. The way he put it was by saying something like, 'Bolivian activities acceptable?' Then there was a box, I think, with a tick or a cross in it. The club I went to was reviewed, and there was a tick in the box, which made sense, because Derek was there every night, selling grams of coke in little wraps made from the pages of glossy magazines. He would then put the little wraps into a cigarette packet; he once told me he could get seventy wraps in one packet, which would represent about £5,000.

So on this particular Monday evening, the day after the article that made it absolutely clear that cocaine was being sold in this club, I walked into this club, and there was Derek, selling cocaine. So I asked him the obvious question. Why were the police not here? If a journalist on a Sunday newspaper could find out where the drug dealers were, just by making a couple of phone calls, why didn't the drug squad, or whatever they were called, men who spent their whole lives trying to track down drug dealers, men who were obsessed, who prowled the streets, night after night, quizzing people, then going back to the squad room and consulting graphs and charts, their wives getting angry with them because they won't come home, guys who are married to the job, who sit alone in bars, frowning, nursing a shot glass of whisky, racking their brains, no detail too insignificant, notebooks bulging . . . why were these guys not here, right now?

More pertinently, why had they never, ever been here?

Why was Derek not quaking in his boots? Did the police know what he was doing?

Of *course* they know what I'm doing, he said. Of *course* they're not stupid. He said he had to pay them a substantial amount of money, regularly. Then they left him alone.

'Right,' I said. I nodded slowly. That was the coming-of-age moment.

Derek said he sometimes had trouble when a new guy arrived on the squad. He said one detective had tried to arrest him at his house in the country. But he called the guy's boss on his mobile phone, and handed the phone over, and the inspector had a word, and the new guy went away, and now they got along fine.

It had always been like this, he said. If you're a criminal, and you have money, you get to know the police, and you work something out. It's the same as the relationship between pharmaceutical companies and governments. Why should it be any different? The one proviso, he said, was that you had to stay in the district you'd paid for, because you can't pay everybody.

Soon after this, he was visiting somebody outside his district. He had two dogs in his car. The dogs started to bark. Somebody called the police because the dogs wouldn't stop barking. The police arrived. It was one guy in a squad car. He looked into Derek's car and saw two little dogs. He also saw a cigarette packet, and then he saw that there was something strange about the cigarette packet.

Derek was sentenced to nine years.

I put the magazine down, by the side of the bed, waiting for the painkiller to do its work, waiting to turn the corner. The walk up the hill will make me feel better. It always does. I'm stressed, and stress makes you ill. I'm middle-aged, and middle age makes you ill. In their book *Why Do People Get Ill?*, which I can see on the shelf by the side of my bed, medical authors Darian Leader and David Corfield give an interesting answer.

Why *do* people get ill? It's not just germs or viruses, they say. That's because you've always got germs and viruses in you. Being ill is not about the sudden appearance of outside attackers. It is more about the appearance of chinks in your defensive armour.

In other words, first you become ill, and *then* the germs or viruses attack you.

By the time they attack you, *you are already ill.*

And at last, with a heavy heart, I get up off the bed. I floss my teeth, the floss catching in the snags. My gums bleed. A Pyrrhic victory.

I gargle and spit.

Then I check that I've switched all the lights off, that I've switched the cooker off, that I've turned the taps off, trying to quell the panic rising in my chest, a panic I'm familiar with.

One therapist told me this is known as 'catastrophising',

imagining that terrible things are going to happen, that your house will burn down, that it will flood, that you will leave the taps running. Your brain makes you imagine terrible things in order to block out other terrible things that are far more likely, like everyday misery and the slow grind towards death.

I check the taps and I check the stove.

I check the stove and I check the taps.

Everything is fine, fine.

I'm feeling slightly better.

It's just stress.

I'm in the early stages of what the eccentric but brilliant gerontologist Aubrey de Grey calls age-related disease, ageing being, in his opinion, a disease, a curable disease.

And cures, he says, are just around the corner, in the same way that passenger jets, unimaginable to people in the 1930s, filled the skies in the 1960s.

I put my phone in my pocket and my wallet in my pocket and I want to check the stove one more time.

But I don't.

I walk through the door and close the door and fight the urge to go back inside, to go back inside and lie down on the bed and pick up the magazine again and not move for hours. I resist the urge and walk down the stairs.

Towards the hill.

Towards my little boy.

Towards the mother of my little boy.

I walk down the stairs, thinking about the walk.

It will make me feel better.

It always does.

Chapter 3

The sun is shining and the sky is streaky and I walk along the road and up the hill, past the house at the bottom of the hill that I considered buying thirteen years ago, and now it's for sale again, at exactly three times the price it was then.

I'm a writer.

Thirteen years ago, I made the same rate, per word, as I do now.

I look at the house.

It's still the same house. Same tile cladding, same terrace in front, same deceptively small interior. I went in there the other day. The woman showed me round. The place hasn't changed. I could have bought it thirteen years ago. But I can't afford it now. It's worth three times what it was worth thirteen years ago, while every word I write is worth exactly the same as it was worth thirteen years ago.

No, that's wrong, isn't it? The words I write are worth *less*, on account of houses being more expensive.

Why?

Why are houses so much more expensive?

And why has the value of words not increased at the same exponential rate? There must be a mechanism that explains this. Just like there's a mechanism that makes, say, a gun work, or a car, or a plane, or a vacuum cleaner – or, for that matter, the internet.

But I've been on this planet forty-seven years, and I still don't understand how things work. I'm like that guy Donald Rumsfeld – my universe is divided into the things I don't know, and the things I don't know I don't know. For me, as for Rumsfeld, there are known unknowns, and then there's the rest – the unknown unknowns, the planets and galaxies I can't even imagine, let alone see.

I sort of know how Rumsfeld works, though. One thing he does is scare the public by telling them that mad foreigners are highly likely to kill them. Then he takes massive liberties. I suppose I should say I know how Rumsfeld *worked*, because he's retired now, another piece of my past fading into the background, like Thatcher and Reagan and the first George Bush, and, soon, the second George Bush. What a *shocking* thought – that George Bush, the younger Bush, a President I'm only just getting used to, a President I have yet to 'work out', is about to fade into the background. Is he smart? Is he dumb? I still don't know. He could be dumb, or dumb-ish, at the core, with a layer of smartness, a sort of Texan rich-kid bullying smartness, closer to the surface, and then a layer of fresh dumbness actually on the surface. Does he know where the bodies are buried? I think probably not. I think Rumsfeld knows *that* bodies are buried, that great liberties have been taken, that lies have been told, and I think that Rumsfeld's genius is that he aspires to a type of higher ignorance, or studied amnesia. Rumsfeld is brilliant at not knowing things he knew, at severing the connections in his brain between different pieces of information, at creating dead zones in his memory, zones of deniability. So Rumsfeld does not actually lie; he's smart enough to continually rewire his brain. Or rather, he was smart enough, for four decades; I think he started slipping towards the end. (Those comments about 9/11, that there 'had been warnings', and that a 'missile' had damaged the Pentagon, spring to mind.) But Bush, I think, is not in the same class as Rumsfeld. Sure, he knows there's a lot he doesn't know, and the bullying part of him works hard at telling himself he's above these considerations. He is imperial. But is he also full of self-doubt and bottled mania? He's an ex-alcoholic, after all. And his close family, his father and brothers, particularly ultra-smart Neil, must make fun of the dumb side of him. There may be a black well of pure rage and bitterness behind those simian-close eyes. But what do I know? Soon it won't seem to matter anyway, because he'll be history.

Like his father.

Like Thatcher.

Like Reagan.

Reagan! The mystery of *his* dumbness hung over the world like a cloud; I believe it affected people in strange ways. What did it tell us about the Western way of life, that, for eight years its most powerful proponent might be singularly lacking in the one quality we supposedly prize above all others?

I once saw Reagan in the flesh, just after he had stopped being President, in a restaurant in Beverly Hills; when he came in everybody craned their necks, not something people in Beverly Hills usually do, even when it's Tom Hanks or even Tom *Cruise* – usually, they affect disinterest and look downwards, at their prawns, their angel-hair pasta.

But I could tell something was up just by looking at the angle of people's necks. There was craning. People felt that it was okay to crane. Reagan was walking in, cheerfully bustling in, with an entourage, four men in grey suits, and two or three men in paler jackets and trousers, and what struck me was how animated he looked, how unlike the impression I'd had from his presidential addresses on television. This was, I think, 1992, and he must have been into his Alzheimer's by then. So how could he appear smarter, when he was suffering from dementia, than he had on TV years before, when he was, at the very least, at an earlier stage of dementia, or even not demented at all?

To a certain extent, the public dumbness, the TV dumbness, must have been faked. It must have developed along with his political career, as learned behaviour – not quite a ploy, but more a tendency, apparent dumbness fostering success, and therefore a happier White House generally, which in turn would have cemented something deep in Reagan's unconscious that favoured dumbness, which would have caused more happiness around him, more smiling henchmen, nobody ever quite telling him out loud to appear dumb, the dumb show instead *emerging*, which is how most things in the world happen, according to Steven Johnson, who wrote a book about precisely this, called *Emergence*.

So Reagan *seemed* really dumb before the dementia struck, and then *actually got* dumb afterwards, causing an apparently seamless progression. What I might have been seeing in the restaurant was a man at the start of his decline – not as smart as he had been, but not yet as dumb as his TV persona.

Another reason for Reagan not seeming dumb: many people suffering from Alzheimer's disease lose their mental faculties in an inconsistent, up-and-down fashion, an Alpine-looking graph, sliding downwards for months, and then momentarily gaining cognitive function as their neurons stumble upon new connections. The author Jonathan Franzen, writing about his father's decline into Alzheimer's, said that his father, deep into the Alzheimer's endgame, having been incoherent for months, managed to collect his thoughts for long enough one day to write a postcard, something like three sentences strung together, on the

102

subject of his dementia, an incredible feat at the time. This is just like that thing some ten-month-old babies do when they surprise everybody with a full sentence (such as 'I done a poo-poo!') and then go back to being incoherent for weeks and weeks afterwards.

So maybe Reagan, having waded through tangled neurons for months, felt suddenly lucid on this occasion – an unusual outing on a bright, sunny day lifting his spirits. Or maybe an outing was arranged because of the sudden lifting of his mood. Either of these things is possible.

Sitting in the restaurant, looking at the smiling, gesticulating, ruddy-faced Reagan, I decided to walk up to him and shake his hand and say something. I wanted to meet Reagan. Or rather, I wanted to say I'd met Reagan; I wanted to graft a meeting with Reagan on to my personal history. I wanted to add a tiny bit of significance to my life, to collect the sort of handshake my grandson might mention at college sixty or eighty years later, in the same way that I might have mentioned it if my grandfather had shaken hands with FDR or Eisenhower.

I also wanted to look into his eyes, to exchange banter, to come away with a central truth about this man – and, therefore, about the Western world.

How dumb *was* he?

How dumb were we?

I sat there, staring at him. He was laughing and joking. He looked somewhere between not-dumb and not-at-all-dumb. He looked, in fact, like an older version of the shady characters he'd played in the later stages of his movie career, the wearers of black hats he'd portrayed after his facial features, as Martin Amis memorably put it, 'cragged up'. He'd played goodies, then goodies in trouble, then baddies. But now, he'd turned another corner – his age had the effect of making him look *less* bad. As he moved his arms and his eyes, he looked kind – or, rather, *kindly*, a sort of kindness by default, the kindness you dole out when you have less vitality, and therefore less choice.

I got up from my table and started walking towards Reagan's table. Immediately, two of the men in suits perked up. There was twitching in the arm and shoulder areas. I had alerted them. They must have had guns. When I got to within two yards of the table, I inwardly crumbled. I could not think of what to say, could not coordinate myself. So I carried on walking, stumbling now, until I reached the men's room, which was behind Reagan's table. I went into the men's room and tried to calm down. Then I came back out, and walked past Reagan again, and sat back down at my table.

They were watching me. But I knew I would try again. I sat and picked at the cheesecake crumbs on my plate. I waited. Then I had a rush of confidence, and got up, and again made my way towards Reagan's table. Again, the men perked up. Again, I inwardly crumbled. I moved jerkily past the table and went into the men's room. I stood in the men's room, looking in the mirror, looking at my thirty-two-year-old face in the mirror. I was sweating and slightly red.

After about five minutes, I had enough confidence to come out of the men's room. I walked back to my table and sat down. I felt sick. I looked at Reagan. He was moving his hands. One of Reagan's men was looking at me. I began to think that if I walked up to the table again, he would take out his gun.

Bang! My reverie is broken. Now I'm thinking about guns, as I walk up the hill, the concrete path having given way to mud and twigs. Guns. You pull the trigger and a projectile shoots out. There is a controlled explosion, an explosion in a confined space, which releases energy, which *pushes* the projectile out.

The explosion is caused by the effect of percussion on gunpowder. Gunpowder releases energy when you . . .

When you hit it?

I guess it does. I guess it must. It must be chemically unstable. That's how a gun works.

But how does a car work?

You turn the key, which causes a controlled explosion, which forces the wheels to go round.

Oh.

So a car is, essentially, a gun on wheels. Or rather, a car is an ingenious combination – it's both gun and bullet simultaneously; it has to be, otherwise you'd start the car, and the car would shoot along the road on its own, leaving you behind. A car, essentially, is a self-firing bullet, on a large scale, with wheels and a passenger seat, and, if you're very lucky, a walnut dashboard.

Maybe I know more than I think. How does a plane work, then? Well, there's a pilot, who turns the key, and there's a controlled explosion . . . so a plane is a self-firing bullet with a propeller – or alternatively a jet engine, a bunch of pretty girls pushing trolleys, and some Adam Sandler movies.

I only know about planes, though, because I know about vacuum cleaners. A few years ago, I bought a Dyson vacuum cleaner, and it broke, causing a lot of domestic problems. I was in the difficult relationship I mentioned with the woman who wanted our place to look like what I defined as very mid-nineties, although she defined the look as timeless. This was the fourth woman that I lived with, but didn't settle down with. I didn't want to settle down, didn't want to get married, didn't want to jump so quickly into my future.

I wanted my future to be a long way in front of me.

For a long time, I didn't want to stop being young, because I felt that being young had only worked out for a very brief period, and I wanted to recreate that brief period. I wanted to go back and find it again, and do it better. But the more I looked, the harder it was to find. It was pathetic. One of the bad things about getting older is that you start to see things *less* clearly than you did before. You wouldn't think it, but it's true.

Anyway, we bought a Dyson vacuum cleaner. I thought the Dyson would be good, because it did not have a bag, it was 'bag-free', which meant that it was not subject to the laws of diminishing returns – like, say, coal mines are. With a coal mine, you drill a hole – a mineshaft – into a seam of coal, and then you hack some coal out of the seam, put the coal into a bucket, and hoist the bucket to the surface. That's the easiest bucket of coal you'll get from that shaft. The more coal you dig, the further away the seam is from the shaft; eventually, your journey to the coalface gets too long to be worth the candle, so what do you do? You abandon the mineshaft. And then it fills up with water, and years later miners in a new mine will be drilling into a coalface and they'll break through into the old mine, you've read these stories, haven't you, it's 'the old Harrison mine', and the guys are trapped as the water rises around them, leaving maybe a couple of feet of air above them, an 'air pocket', and they pray, and talk about their wives. You only find out about the praying and wife-talking afterwards.

Anyway, there they are, stuck. But there's a local guy, an engineering genius, and he sits up all night and works out where to dig. And the trucks arrive, and guys drill an air hole, and, later, they haul the miners up to the surface, where they are greeted by the wives, the children, and by Hollywood producers looking for a heart-warming story, and later still they get rich and unhappy and start to hate each other and then get divorced, their spirits broken, sitting alone in bars – trapped, you see, trapped by fame and money just as surely as they were trapped in that tunnel.

God, I hate tunnels. I'm claustrophobic. I'm like Charles Bronson's character in *The Great Escape*, the guy who panics when he sees signs that the tunnel is collapsing. Or rather, I'm not, because the point about Bronson's character is that he's brave, he's a hero, one of those Poles who joined the RAF, the ones the old guy in the hotel loved, and his claustrophobia is depicted as a contrast to the heroism. It's out of character.

Whereas I'm cowardly, so my claustrophobia is absolutely in character.

This is something I thought might change as I got older. I thought I'd grow out of the claustrophobia. I used to look at older guys, with their slumpy shoulders and their creased faces, and did not imagine that they were afraid of things like enclosed spaces; I sort of saw their wrinkles and bad posture not as signs of weakness, but as armour, which turned out to be totally wrong.

I've had the claustrophobia as long as I can remember. When I was eleven, the kids in my year were invited to put their names forward for the annual tour of the town's sewers. You didn't have to put your name down, and I shouldn't have. But it was traditional to put your name down, and hope that you were one of the lucky few who got chosen for the trip down the sewers. So I put my name down, because I did not want to lose face, hoping that it would not come up. Of course, it did. I was one of the 'lucky ones'.

Again, I didn't formulate a proper, workable plan to deal with the situation. Instead, I adopted a new policy, pretending to myself that the ominous date was not on the horizon, was not creeping towards me. On the day itself, I went to school as usual. The sewer party, including me, set off after morning assembly.

One boy said, 'I've heard you have to go hundreds of feet underground and then climb up a wall of shit.'

I felt like I was going to vomit with fear – not because of the wall of shit, but because of the horrifying combination of being simultaneously underground and high up. So I went straight to the teacher and told him that I'd had a change of heart. He tried to persuade me to go down. I hate those conversations, when somebody is trying to persuade you to do something you don't want to do, and both of you cannot quite articulate your positions. He could not allay my fears, and knew it; I could not be persuaded, but did not know why. The conversation must have gone something like this:

Him: 'It's perfectly safe.'

Me: 'But it's *underground*.'

Him: 'It's a sewer. A sewer is underground.'

Then the teacher said something that really hurt: 'You don't know how lucky you are. Do you know how many boys would give anything for a chance to go into these sewers?'

I did not go down. Instead, I sat on the pier, on a bench, looking out to sea, trying to imagine what would happen when the other boys came out of the sewer, and, worse, when the boys who had been in the sewer got back to school, there now being two distinct categories of boys who had set out on the original trip: sewer-denizens, i.e. everybody else, and sewer virgins, i.e. me.

It was going to be a living hell.

I had been told to wait on a bench by the pier. I tried to read my pop music magazine, but my fingers were too cold to hold it for long. I went across the road and bought a cup of coffee and went back to the pier and sat on the bench and drank my coffee and waited for the others to come out of the sewer.

*   *   *

I don't know, for sure, what it is about tunnels that I hate. It's not a Freudian sex thing. I don't hate the idea of vaginas, regret my time in the womb, or anything like that.

But then again, if I did, it would be on an unconscious level. So maybe I do.

Do I find the idea of vaginas terrifying? For a second I try to concentrate, try to think about vaginas. Are they scary? Would there have been any time when . . .

My God! I suppose, if I think about it, some of the most nerve-racking moments in your life happen when you first begin to encounter vaginas, when you are a teenager, when your response to the vagina will either be a huge success or a terrible meltdown. And even if you don't have terrible meltdowns, the fear alone must be hugely significant. So maybe, on an unconscious level, all guys have a fear of vaginas.

But then, not all guys are claustrophobic, are they?

So maybe some guys don't have scary vaginal moments as teenagers.

Oh, really? Come *on*.

Of course they do. Just about the coolest guy I knew as a teenager told me he'd got into a terrible situation. He'd paired off with a girl, they'd found a bedroom at a party, he'd been drunk, he'd got to the point of the offering of the vagina, that was how he put it, a question of something being offered, and somehow, the wrestle with the condom and his drunkenness had ganged up, and he hadn't been able to get an erection. Still, the girl had been good about it, and they tried again, and he was very nervous, so nervous he'd felt the need for a few steadying drinks.

Again, he failed.

That's when he told me the story, after the second failure. He had arranged a third meeting. Success would depend on a near-impossible feat of logistics. This, he felt, was his last opportunity.

Another failure and he would be too damaged to carry on. He had to keep calm, keep smiling, find a quiet, parent-free spot, drink just the right amount, catch the wave of his libido before it was frozen out by the icy fingers of fear that, he knew, would try to invade his mind and body at the crucial moment.

The worst thing, he said, was the fact that he'd got so close. So very close.

'You should have seen it,' he said. 'It was right . . . *there*. And I couldn't do anything about it.'

Maybe some people are fine, not riven with anxiety, and of course guilt, the guilt driving the anxiety. Maybe some guys are not struck dumb. Jesus! I can remember probably one of the best moments of my teenage life, at the age of sixteen, at a party; I found a friend of mine in an upstairs bedroom with a girl, and not just a girl, but the girl everybody lusted after and dreamed of, and this guy was drunk, and soon he started jabbering and collapsed, the whole thing being too much for him, and in a dream-like sequence of events, I started kissing the girl, and we got into the bed, and some stuff happened, but not much, and guys came into the room, and caught us, which was the best thing I could imagine. Better to be caught in bed with this girl, having done not much, that to have done some more and not got caught. We made a date, me and this girl, at a pizza restaurant.

One guy said to me, 'This is *it*. That pussy is *yours*.'

But in the restaurant I did not feel ready, could not think of anything to say. We sat there, each mouthful of pizza a relief from the dumbstruck non-pizza moments between mouthfuls. I felt like the guy in *The Loneliness of the Long Distance Runner*, one of my favourite books at the time. I didn't know why I didn't want to finish the race, but I didn't want to finish the race.

We had no dessert.

Outside the restaurant, I said, 'Shall I . . . you know? Walk you, uh, to the, uh, uh, the, um, bus stop?'

'Don't worry,' she said.

So to say that I was not afraid of vaginas can't be strictly true.

I guess I must have been terrified. The first time I actually had sex, I was eighteen. I felt it was really, really late; I thought that if I did not do it soon, I might never do it, might be permanently jinxed. I'd had several near-misses. The night it happened, the girl clearly set out to seduce me, and there were moments of fear, which turned into moments close to horror, mixed of course with excitement, as the girl took her clothes off, and then when everything worked, when I knew I was not going to fail to get an erection, my sense of relief almost put me in shock, almost drugged me, the whole thing working on a level of consciousness that made it seem, in retrospect, like footage I was watching, not pornographic, not dirty, but grainy and blurred, mostly shadows, and of course I didn't use a condom, of course I was not capable of making that sort of decision. I had the young man's quick orgasm, and followed it with the young man's ability to continue as if nothing had happened; when I had a second orgasm, minutes later, I faked the fact that it was not the first, and then my mind got to work with the business of rewriting the history of the event, downplaying the terror, the horror, the dim lights, the jerky shadows on the ceiling, the robotic moves, the close-run victory over panic. The next morning I sneaked into this memory like a burglar and carefully replaced everything with new details – of furniture and clothes, of hair and breasts, of the orgasm, of the entire narrative, from start to finish, making it happen more slowly and deliberately, more like a gourmet meal and less like a crime or a battle.

*   *   *

111

About a week after this I went to visit my father in his Nova
Scotian house-in-the-woods, thinking the girl was pregnant,
because she told me she was, in an effort I think to stop me
from going to Canada, and it was there, in the Canadian house,
that I damaged my shoulder, sliding down the stairs, something I
would not have done under normal circumstances, but these
were not normal circumstances, because I thought I'd got somebody pregnant, which was weirdly terrifying, or rather which
was of course terrifying, but also more weird than you'd think; it
made me see things, like trees or whatever, as if they were in an
alternate universe. One morning my father left me in the house,
left me to drink coffee and relax, while he went off somewhere. I
did not relax. I slid down the stairs, and landed badly, damaging
my shoulder for ever, an injury that still hurts now, the ball still
slides out of my shoulder socket when I carry a heavy suitcase,
and when I think about this I always think of one particular
moment when the ball fell out of the socket, in a lift, in a hotel in
Los Angeles, when I was thirty-seven. I was checking out of the
hotel, holding a heavy suitcase. The other person in the lift was a
guy my age, a minor rock star I'd once written something rude
about, Ian something, he sang in a band called the Cult, and I
remember thinking he looked good for his age, was ageing better
than me, me with my paunch, my red face, my innard pain, me
with the ball slipping out of my shoulder socket.

Just after I'd written the rude thing about this guy, during a
period of promiscuity when I was twenty-six, I went to see a
band one night, worried about the fact that this was probably
the seventh day in a row that I'd been suffering from an itchy
lump in my groin. The lump burst, and almost immediately my
genital area was suffused with biting insects. I was being bitten
simultaneously by hundreds of blood-sucking crab lice. When I
looked, the lice appeared as a cloud, or maybe a flock of tiny

birds in a forest as seen from a very high vantage. I ran back to a friend's house, and tried to get rid of the tiny bugs by combing them out with an aluminium comb, a fine-tooth comb, and crushing them on the side of the bath. I was at it for half the night. I killed hundreds. But they kept on coming. They were like the hordes of warriors in the film *Zulu*. I combed and crushed, hour after hour, while they sang their warrior songs and waited for the real battle to begin. The next day, I went to a clinic where the doctor looked at me and then asked for a favour. He had a group of medical students, he said, and these students would really appreciate it if they could have a look at my crab lice. 'It's not often you get a case like this,' he told me. The lice had really dug in. They had colonised me. Pretty soon, they would suck me dry. Then, like the Greenland Norse and the Easter Islanders, they would have to leave the only world they knew and find somewhere else to live.

I agreed to the doctor's request. I lay back, trousers down, and closed my eyes, and listened to the voices of the medical students. They all sounded very serious. I went away with a jar of lotion the colour and consistency of semen, which was supposed to kill the bugs. The biting became sporadic, and then occasional, and after about thirty days it had stopped altogether.

Of course, Shakespeare was terrified of vaginas, wasn't he? Just look at sonnet 129, in which he compares the general greed of mankind with the male lust for vaginas. They mess with your head, he says. You lust after things, including vaginas, until you've got them, and then you realise you didn't want them as much as you thought you did. That's more or less his position.

In any case, I don't think my fear of tunnels is *all* about vaginas. I think some of it is just about tunnels. I was once stuck in a tunnel in an underground train that was on fire, or rather the rubber brake pads were smouldering, but the train was filling up with smoke, and people were moving from the front of the train, where the smoke was, to the back of the train, where I was, and they were opening the doors, so all the carriages were filling up with smoke, and as I sat in my seat, I was full of panicky anger and self-blame, an appalling combination, because I'd smelled the burning rubber smell two stops before, and I'd toyed with the idea of getting off, but I had not got off, because I did not want to seem eccentric – after all, nobody else was getting off. I had a core emotion of pure conservatism, a sense that I had to stick with the programme, a sense that getting off would be letting others down, spreading panic, not getting on with the business of tunnelling through the city. And when my carriage filled with smoke and people, enough people to crush me, I was furious, the fury stoking the panic and the terror. I was furious that I'd let this inner conservatism predominate, against my better judgement, and later, after the train had crawled into the next station, and we'd got out, coughing, I stood on the escalator, and rose towards the surface, inwardly shuddering, and the thing I'll never forget is the feeling of wanting to cry when, still on the escalator, I saw a little patch of blue sky.

Perhaps I also hate tunnels because they tell us something about our greed, or our impatience – they are there because we need to burn rocks to feed our famished power stations, or because we can't be bothered to go around a mountain, but need to go through it, because we're in such a hurry, or because there's something underground and we need to know about it, or find it. Isn't this why mining disasters make us shudder? Isn't it because the trapped guys shouldn't be down there in the first place? They are an example of man's hubris, like the astronauts in the movie *Apollo 13* – or rather, like the real-life astronauts in Apollo 13, who got stuck up there, sitting in the capsule as the air leaked out.

And now I remember a story I read about some trapped miners, and how it made me feel sick with dread, how it recreated the feelings I'd had in the underground train; I remember reading about the low tunnel, the beams, the constant possibility of collapse, the underground rain and even fog, and the miners' steamy breath in the cold air. I remember that when the miners broke through into the abandoned mine, unleashing a torrent of sulphurous water, the seam they were mining was *five miles* from the original mineshaft.

But the bag-free Dyson, unlike an ordinary vacuum cleaner, was not like a mineshaft. The thing about an ordinary vacuum cleaner with a bag is that it sucks air, and dirt, through the bag. It is, essentially, a bag with a propeller at one end and a straw at the other. The propeller sucks air – and dirt – through the straw, and into the bag. But this means that every bit of dirt entering the bag makes the ordinary vacuum cleaner less effective – it is destroyed by its own success.

Like a coal mine, it operates on a law of diminishing returns.

That's why James Dyson invented the bag-free vacuum cleaner. It was a great idea – just like the 'ball-barrow', another Dyson invention, which is a wheelbarrow with a ball instead of a wheel at the front.

I thought that the new vacuum cleaner would ease some of the strain in my relationship with the woman who, as I saw it, believed that the fashions of 1994 were timeless. I somehow associated clean carpets and dust-free floorboards with domestic harmony. But it really didn't work that way. For one thing, the Dyson clogged up. It got jammed. For a while, it limped on, making a strange croaky noise, like an old man who has smoked all his life. And then – nothing. No suck.

Our arguments got worse. A layer of dust built up in the flat. I was drinking heavily and snorting coke. My bowels were in serious decline. A lump had recently appeared on my leg. I was thirty-nine years old. Whenever I looked at the bagless vacuum cleaner, I felt a rising sense of anger.

Then a newspaper asked me if I wanted to interview James Dyson. I took a taxi to his house. I brought along my bag-free, but clogged, Dyson vacuum cleaner. It was a warm day. I was brutally hung-over. I must have reeked of stale booze, of the dismal last-chance saloon I'd tumbled out of a few hours before. When Dyson opened the door, I asked him to mend my vacuum cleaner.

He was a tall, grey-haired man in his fifties. He hadn't really made it big until he was middle-aged. The ball-barrow had not been a world-beater. Anyway, he loved the idea of mending my vacuum cleaner. He took it apart and ferreted around inside. That was when he explained how planes work. When a propeller turns, it sucks air towards it. A vacuum cleaner, when you think about it, is just a plane in a cave. Dyson also told me that a jet engine is really just lots of propellers in a tube. I thought a jet engine would be more complicated than that. But it's just propellers in a tube. I knew that Frank Whittle had invented it, and that when he thought of the concept his boss had told him not to be so ridiculous. But apparently if you put propellers in a tube the suck is magnified hugely, hence the ability to carry two hundred passengers and their luggage, and even my friend Mark's body, in the hold, hence the flocks of birds that get minced up, and hence global warming, with all the jet trails. And here's something creepy. After 9/11, people measuring air temperature in the United States recorded three of the warmest September days ever, and this was because these were the only days without jets in the sky, without jet trails reflecting the sun's rays back out into space.

And you know what was blocking my bagless vacuum cleaner? Shit. It was shit, from my girlfriend's rabbit. Shit, and carpet fibre, and sawdust soaked with rabbit urine. Really stinky. James

116

Dyson tipped it all out on his carpets, and Hoovered it, or rather Dysoned it, all up again.

I'm walking faster now, getting into a good rhythm. Calm down, I tell myself. I can feel the first ominous signs of my mind beginning to unravel. Moving closer to my destination, closer to the mother of my little boy and my little boy, I can feel myself becoming very slightly unhinged.

I walk rhythmically, thinking about the fundamental facts of life. Everything falls apart. But that's fine. Everything falls apart because it's *supposed* to fall apart. Scientifically speaking, the real wonder is that things hold together at all. Falling apart is just what things do. By things, I mean things in general.

I'm trying not to think of my relationship.

I'm trying to think of anything but my relationship.

Sometimes, things look like they're going to hold together for ever – like, say, the Beatles around the time of *Rubber Soul*, or the TV series *Friends* after about three seasons, or *Frasier* at its height, or the capitalist way of life in the middle of the last century.

A good example of this is Bill Bryson's lovely account of growing up in Middle America in the 1950s and the 1960s, *The Life and Times of the Thunderbolt Kid*. Born in 1949, he lived in a nice house in a good suburb of a medium-sized city in the richest country on earth at the exact moment when capitalism looked like it might last for ever. He and his family had big cars and huge fridges and ice-cream sundaes when these things actually made people happy, and this was because people were having these things for the first time. Abundance is magnificent when it's a novelty, when it follows austerity. What nobody understood was that, pretty soon, abundance would lead to boredom and decadence and envy and self-loathing, and that

117

banks, backed by governments, would instinctively understand this, and would stoke the fires of abundance, lending everybody money to buy more and more things – which would not make them happy, but miserable. Now, of course, capitalism looks like a busted flush, although it will be a long, wretched time before we all admit it.

But imagine being born in 1949, and being, say, twelve years old, and walking through your suburb, past the endless lawns, the endless drives with their big, finned cars, the endless swimming pools. I once read that Khrushchev, the Russian President, had flown over to America for some summit in the early sixties, and he'd got in his plane and flown back, and as the plane took off he looked out of the window and saw the swimming pools in the back gardens, a pool in each garden, a view you don't see from the street, and this, he said later, was the moment he knew that Communism would not prevail.

John Cheever, who lived in the suburbs, had a more nuanced view of suburban swimming pools. Guiltily bisexual, alcoholic, and generally self-loathing, he saw something in swimming pools that an envious outsider like Khrushchev could never have seen. In Cheever's story 'The Swimmer', published in 1964, a middle-aged man lounges poolside at a suburban Sunday barbecue and wonders if it would be possible to get from where he is to his own, similar detached house-and-pool combo, not in the usual way, not by road, but by swimming. So he hops over the fence and embarks on the journey. It's several miles. He swims across each pool he comes to. On the way, he imagines arriving home, imagines the look on his wife's face, imagines his lovely children, and he keeps hopping over the fences and jumping in the pools. But, as he gets closer to home, things begin to change, at first almost imperceptibly. Leaves start to fall. The sky darkens. When he arrives, he finds his house boarded up, his family nowhere to be seen.

118

You think: he's lost everything!

And then you think: he never really had anything in the first place.

It was *lost all along*.

Incidentally, the first dead person I saw was in a swimming pool. It was 1972; I was twelve. I'm not sure whether the guy was dead when I first saw him, or whether he died in the course of the next few minutes. He was big and fit-looking, a twenty-four-year-old German research scientist, specialising in snail-borne tropical diseases. He was floating, face down, in an open-air swimming pool.

I had come to the pool with my friend Tim. My mother had given us a lift. The pool, owned by the local university, was at an off-campus site in the middle of a wood, open to faculty members and their families. We lived close to the university, on an estate built to house university staff. On a hot morning in the summer, the neighbours were always going to the pool; you could always get a ride. You could knock on doors and find a ride within minutes. Afterwards, you did not have to go back with the people you came with. In my memory, somebody always had room in the car for you. So I went to the pool a lot.

The people who lived in the village were all around the same age. The fathers were born in 1930 or 1932; the mothers in 1933 or 1937 – roughly speaking. So in 1972 the mothers were in their mid-thirties. About half of them wore bikinis, half wore one-piece swimsuits. There was a pool, a lake, a wood, a sports hall with nothing in it, and some chalets. It never quite got crowded. There were two slightly ragged tennis courts.

You walked up a bank, a grassy mound, towards the pool, and this is where my memory starts.

There is the mound-like bank.

People are getting out of the pool.

I can't make out what is being said.

I see the guy.

For some reason, people are not getting the guy.

They are leaving the guy.

Face down.

The ambulance arrives. A paramedic wades in. He must wade in. But the sequence in my mind is confused. I have no picture of the paramedic wading in. The next thing: the guy is out of the pool. He is slumped. I am horrified and entranced. I am standing next to Tim. We are both regulars at the pool. Both our fathers work at the university. My father's field is psychology.

Tim's father's field is snail-borne tropical diseases.

Tim's father goes on trips to Africa, and when he gets back he always hosts a slide show for the neighbours. He is serious about his work; for the slide show we sit in Tim's parents' darkened sitting room, looking at projected pictures of the surfaces of sub-Saharan waterholes. I remember somebody asking what the slides were pictures of.

'Snail environments,' Tim's father said.

So when the paramedic turns the drowned guy's body over, in order to begin what will be a failed effort to resuscitate him, Tim recognises him.

He says something like: 'Jesus! It's Jürgen!'

The drowned guy is, and suddenly *was*, Tim's father's re-search assistant.

Later we go for a walk in the woods. We are trying to ascertain something about Jürgen. Did he look dead? We agree that he did. I am more excited than I am horrified. But Jürgen did not really look dead at all. He looked like a healthy young athlete, dripping wet and lying down. There was something I could not grasp about his death. It had surprised me, certainly, but it did not seem to have traumatised me. So this was death? The man had dived in and hit his head on some underwater steps. He had lost consciousness and swallowed water.

The weirdest thing was that, for a long time, this was a happy memory – a sunny happening from my youth, like the time a tugboat let loose a cargo of oranges in the harbour. The boxes of oranges floated to the pier, and we hauled some of the boxes out, and got them home in somebody's dad's station wagon. That was the day of the oranges. This was the day of the dead guy. I was there. I was glad I was there. I still am, weirdly. At some point in my forties, though, the memory darkened. I began to think of the guy's parents, and his unborn children, who possibly would have sat in a darkened room in Düsseldorf or somewhere, while he did slide shows of *Sneckenumgebungen*. Snail environments.

He would be pushing sixty.

The second dead person I saw was my grandfather in his coffin.

The third, fourth and fifth dead people I saw were the victims of a road accident in south London in 1986. It was around dusk on a winter evening. I was on a bus, and the bus stopped, and I sat there, reading, and when I looked up, the street was full of buses – the cars had all turned back. I got out and walked. Up ahead was a flashing light, eerie in the distance, and as I approached it I saw a uniformed policeman running towards me. He stopped by a wall and vomited over the wall. He was crying. The flashing light was an ambulance. A truck had smashed into a car and crushed it against a wall. Bodies and body parts had been removed from the car. They were on the road. There was an arm. I went home, and the next day, in the evening, I met my father, who remarked that I was not looking well.

'I saw an accident,' I said.

I was amazed, because it was the evening, and I had not thought of the bodies all day.

The sixth dead person I saw was a teenage girl. She came out of a public toilet and fell on the ground. She was twitching. Somebody called an ambulance. I could hear the siren coming closer. A paramedic put a clear mask over the girl's mouth. But he could not resuscitate her. An overdose of drugs, I suppose.

The seventh dead person I saw was an old woman in a mortuary. I was interviewing an undertaker. He offered to show me around the building. When he got to the place where he kept the dead people, he asked me if I wanted a look. He said he thought there was one dead person in there. There was. It was an old woman. She was wrapped up in a blanket. He slid her out. We looked at her. I could just see the top of her head and the shape of her body underneath the blanket.

I was in a taxi. The driver was talking about roadworks. He was angry. The damn roadworks, he was saying. The stupid idiots and their stupid roadworks. We saw a blue flashing light ahead. The traffic had slowed right down.

The driver was telling me about a complicated diversion in front of us, and how the people who had organised it had no idea. We went slowly past the flashing light. There was an ambulance. There was a body. Parts of it were crushed, and the leg twisted away at an angle.

For about ten seconds, I wondered if either of us would mention the body. Then I knew that neither of us would.

The driver said, 'Look at that.'

We had drawn level with the roadworks.

He said, 'What did I tell you?'

I was thinking about something else. I was thinking about all the dead people I had seen.

Seven. And now this man.

He was the eighth.

I can feel the sun on my face. I can see the light through the clouds. I can see the hills in the distance, covered with a bluish haze. I'm not feeling too bad, although I can feel the tiredness underneath, the tiredness that follows me around these days. It frightens me, the tiredness. It feels as if it's rising through my stomach and chest, creeping towards my brain stem.

I met a man who had a debilitating illness for twenty years, between the ages of twenty-five and forty-five. When he was cured, he was asked how he felt.

He didn't *feel* cured, he said. He felt tired most of the time.

Someone had to explain to him that this was not tiredness *per se*; this was middle age.

I'm tired because I don't sleep properly. I don't sleep properly because, after the age of forty-five, all bets are off. Why should I sleep properly? Why should anything about me work properly at this age? In the wild, I'd be dead; I'd have been eaten by a predator, or my teeth would have rotted and I'd have starved.

Of course I'm tired. It's perfectly normal.

In the distance I can see the windscreens of cars flashing in the sun. The thought comes to me of being in a car with the mother of my little boy and my little boy, and it's intense, I'm almost *in* the car, can almost project myself back into the past. It's painful. It creeps up on me, this projection; I'll be doing something and then it will come, an unbidden memory of a thing I did in my relationship, a thing *we* did, like going somewhere in the car.

I keep being ambushed.

Will I always be ambushed?

This happens to people, doesn't it? They fall in love, and then the person dumps them, and they never get over it, they never move on; in their mind the relationship never withers, but always stays young, like James Dean; the relationship stays in the memory like James Dean – crisp-featured, ageless, beckoning.

Dead.

Thirty-five years after James Dean died in a car crash, in the week of the anniversary of his death, I went to California to write about the phenomenon of dying young. I wanted to drive Dean's death route, to see the things that Dean had seen in the moments leading up to his death. Also, I wondered who would turn up at the spot where he'd died. My idea was to rent a car similar to the one Dean had driven – a Porsche. But in the rental car lot I had a change of heart, and I rented a big white Volvo instead. Dean had been twenty-four at the time of his last drive.

I was thirty.

I stayed in a hotel in the desert, and drove along the death route five days in a row, trying to time my drive with Dean's. It was a lonely place, out in the desert. You'd go miles without passing anybody. It was oilfields in the southern part of the route, and then cotton fields. Dean died in the cotton fields. One morning I drove through the fields, counting twenty-seven miles between one place and the next. It was close to where Cary Grant had been dive-bombed by the crop-spraying plane in the Hitchcock film *North by Northwest*. It was late September, still pretty hot, and there were strange objects on the road. I couldn't see what they were. I kept running over them.

They were some kind of caterpillar.

I was the only guest at my hotel. I would drive the Dean route, and then go back to the hotel, and drink beer. The sky was clear and it was cold at night, and I would go to bed and have vivid nightmares. I'd read all the Dean stuff, the cult material about the days leading up to his crash, the interview he'd given about road safety, just before the fatal day. I knew he was driving his Porsche towards a race at Salinas, and that he was travelling with his mechanic, a former Nazi Luftwaffe pilot called Rolf Weutherich, who would survive the crash, but then die in another crash twelve years later.

I also looked at the photographs taken just after Dean's death, the pre-dusk shots, taken by Sanford Roth, Dean's personal photographer, a few minutes after the crash. The positioning of shadows gives a clue as to exactly when Dean died, and therefore how fast Dean had been driving. There were photographs of the ambulance, a big old 1950s thing, like a hearse, and people said that if you looked at the picture carefully, you could see Dean's ghost hovering above the vehicle as the stretcher with his body was being loaded inside, and I looked, but I couldn't see the ghost.

I was afraid of it, though. Just looking for it gave me the heebie-jeebies.

Dean had driven into the car of a young farmer named Donald Turnupseed. I spoke to Turnupseed on the phone. I didn't want to, but my editor had insisted. Turnupseed said he did not have any comment, and afterwards I felt guilty about calling him. He was sixty. Dean, had he lived, would have been fifty-nine. Turnupseed hung up on me; it was the way he did that, and the tone of his voice, a sort of wounded resignation, that made me feel guilty. I can't remember how I got his number. He must have been sitting there, in his timber-framed house, steeling himself for the thirty-fifth anniversary.

The night before the anniversary, I went to sleep at around midnight and woke up three hours later. I was having a dream in which I couldn't move, and in which a man was standing above me, with some sort of fabric hanging down from his head. When

I woke up I thought I could see him in the room. I was deeply disturbed. I could not get back to sleep. So I went downstairs to the lobby and watched sports on the ESPN channel and drank coffee from the machine, while the receptionist manned the desk. No guests came or went.

A photographer had arranged to meet me. He turned up at breakfast time. He was a tall, middle-aged guy who told me that he had just recently kidnapped a dog; it was a complicated story and he was not yet reconciled to it. The fact that he had kidnapped this dog was freaking him out. Hysteria was close to the surface. We had breakfast and headed out into the desert, and before long we were driving alongside the Dean cars – the 1950s Oldsmobiles and Cadillacs, big cars, mostly without the fins, because when Dean died, it was still pre-fin. They only started putting the fins on the cars in 1957, so Dean never knew about it. When you think about it, he lived in an austere time.

Again, it was hot. We drove along the route, through the oilfields. We could smell the oil. There were warehouses, pumps, and the silver columns of refineries glinting in the heat-shimmer. The road was pocked and rutted and every so often there were shredded tyres on the hard shoulder.

At the death spot, people were gathering, standing in the heat and pointing at the ground and talking to each other. Some had scrapbooks and albums full of Dean-related items.

I'd worked something out about Dean's death. With twenty-five seconds of conscious life remaining, he'd have been raked in the eye by the setting sun; he was driving over the crest of a hill into the sunset. I'd tried it. As you come over the hill, you are blinded; on the other side of the valley, there's a range of mountains, and at the time of Dean's death the sun is a fiery ball setting behind the ridge of these mountains, which filters the rays in a weird way. Dean would have driven straight into a field of light. And just as his vision came back, he had to swerve to avoid an overtaking car going the other way, which put him into the path of Turnupseed's black and white Ford. Dean's Porsche was flung fifty-five feet. The force of the impact broke his neck.

We parked at a diner up the road from the death spot and walked towards the death spot. I got talking to a guy who had an album of the Sanford Roth photographs. He was a middle-aged postal worker from Boston. He explained his theory: 'Do you know why Dean wasn't thrown clear of the car? It was because he had his foot stuck between the brake and the clutch. It shows he was down-shifting, trying to brake. It shows he'd seen the Ford. The Ford was skidding. It wasn't Jimmy's fault.'

While we were talking about this, a car drove up and skidded to a halt in the dust.

'*Oh* no,' said the mailman. 'I know these guys, and they are *weird*.'

A man got out of the car and ran towards us. He was holding something in his hand. He gave it to me.

'You know what you are holding?'

'No.'

'You know what that is, man?'

'No.'

'You'll never guess, man. It's beautiful. You know what that is? It's a piece of the original Route 66. This, man, is a piece of history. It's a piece of America. Who are you, by the way, and what brings you here?'

'Hi. I'm William. I'm writing about James Dean.'

'You're a writer?'

'Yes.'

'Oh my God. You wait there. You wait there. I have got a story that will blow your head off. This story, man, it will make your career.'

The man jogged to his car, took something out of the car and jogged back. The thing he had taken from the car was a stack of papers.

He was shaking with excitement.

He said, 'Okay. These here are legal papers. Because I'm suing Steven Spielberg. Okay. Who wrote *Back to the Future*?'

'I don't know.'

'Come on, man. Guess!'

'Spielberg?'

'No.'

'I don't know then. Robert Zemeckis?'

'No, no, no. The author of *Back to the Future* is . . . well, you're looking at him.'

'You wrote *Back to the Future*?'

'I can prove it to you. I'm going to tell you something that proves it beyond all doubt. And then you can write my story. Are you interested?'

'Well, I suppose if you could prove it.'

'Don't you believe me?'

'Well, you'd have to prove it.'

'Okay. Here goes. You know the scene in which Marty McFly goes back in time, to the bar, and he goes up to the bar, man, and he orders a "Coke Free"? That's what he says – "I'd like a Coke Free". And the guy behind the bar says, "You can't have a Coke free – it costs 25 cents!"'

'Yes, I know that scene.'

'See, Marty McFly does not want the Coke free, as in free of charge. He wants a Coke Free, as in free of calories. But, but, see – in the 1950s, they did not have Coke, or Pepsi, that was, like, free of calories.'

'Okay.'

'Well, I wrote that scene.'

'Okay.'

128

'Is that not enough?'

'What?'

'Does that not prove to you, beyond all doubt, that I wrote the movie?'

'Well, no.'

'Come on, man.'

'On its own, it's not enough.'

'What are the chances that somebody, other than me, would think of that?'

'I see.'

'I mean, man, they ripped me off *totally*. The time travel, the bar, the *exact same product*. Now, what will a judge say, when Spielberg tries to wriggle out of that?'

So maybe my relationship is like James Dean, and I am like that guy – a nut, a fantasist. And maybe I'll never get any better, or, horribly, maybe I'll get worse, always looking back, looking back.

This actually happened to a friend of mine, a very clever guy who has since turned out to have 'borderline personality' – do you have borderline personality, or do you have *a* borderline personality? I'm not sure. Anyway, this guy's wife dumped him, and he showed me a letter she'd sent him, very brusque, something like 'Never, ever try to contact me again'. It was signed just with her initials and surname.

After I'd read the letter, the dumped guy said, 'What do you think? Personally, I think she's saying she wants me back.'

I looked at him.

He said, 'I think she's left the door open.'

And now, I've been dumped, I'm the dumped guy, and while I'm pretty sure that my dumping is a permanent thing, part of me feels . . .

Oh my God.

Part of me feels that the door might still be open.

When I went round to see the dumped guy, his place . . . well, there were piles of books everywhere, and he was . . .

Oh my God.

What am I going to *do*? That is, if I don't get back with the mother of my little boy? (Which I won't, which I won't, I can feel it in my bones.) Well, I will either be a sad, celibate post-bachelor, wounded and de-fanged, a man of long walks and corduroy, a man who supplies ready quips at social events and quotes famous people, always has a quote at the ready, a man of studied cheerfulness; or I will be a miserable man, wary of women, a man who cooks according to recipes, a man of cellophane baggies in drawers, always having enough tinfoil; or I will be single and permanently ready for action, the ideal of a friend of mine who was in a long-term relationship, and who told me he wished he'd had children, and got his divorce over with, so that he could play the field again; or else I will find a woman who does not want children, and settle down with her in a parody of the pre-children relationships I used to have, possibly having to deal with the dog or cat that sometimes turns up in these relationships. I remember it well, the dog or cat, or rather the dog and the cats, there were several cats, I only ever liked one cat, but I remember being in a relationship that started to go wrong, we began to drift apart, it was as if we were seeing each other for the first time, now that we had some distance, and I don't think she liked me, and during this awkward period we saw a notice in a window about a lost cat, and the picture on the notice looked very like a cat that came into our garden, and we started to try to lure the cat into the house, and the cat was very shy, very wary, this whole thing took ages, and one time we got the cat into the house but couldn't catch it, it was running all over, and we got scratched, but we got more and more determined, and one day we caught the cat and put it in a box, and called the number on the notice, and took the cat to the person at the end of the phone, and she opened the box, preparing for a moment of great happiness, but it was not to be, the cat was the wrong cat, and we split up soon afterwards; or I will find a woman who does not want children, but who wants an organised, adult relationship, each with our own places, a relationship with elaborately planned foodie holidays in France and Italy, a 'we always book with this or that website' relationship; or I'll have a 'friendship with benefits', in which we will spend ages discussing our past sex lives with no jealousy, or else jealousy will creep up and spoil what was a good friendship; or I'll have a relationship with a woman who has children, or possibly one child, and we'll form a strange but workable family unit at the weekends, me with my lovely, boisterous son, who looks like me, very like me, except for the fact that he's got blond hair, she with her son or daughter, possibly of a similar or compatible age; or I'll find a younger woman, who has not had children but wants them, and against the odds I'll fall in love, and she with me, and we'll have our own child, her first and my second, and I'll tell her all about what you do when you're pregnant, and about hospitals, and she will be annoyed by this, but try not to show it, or maybe she will have a moment of anger, yelling at me in the hospital's parking lot when I tell her about the parking procedures, or the way to alert the nurses, or the quick way to the maternity ward, and then at weekends my son will live with us, and she will think he's my special child, and of course he will be, that's all I can think at the moment, parents of one child being unable to imagine loving a second child as much as the first, this whole issue being more complicated when the mother of the second child is different from the mother of the first; or I'll be a serial shagger, a lothario, honing my skills, developing my lines, my gestures, prowling my hunting grounds, giving books of poetry as sleazy gifts, knowing about condom machines and eventually Viagra, and of course Cialis, which is slightly different from Viagra. I once saw an older man, a man in his fifties, exit a restaurant lavatory in what looked like a hurry, and I went in after him and he'd left a Viagra packet and an emptied foil-and-plastic suppository container, whatever that was for, a double hit of some kind, getting him ready for the evening's performance; and might this be me, in just a few years, dick pills at the ready and a torpedo up my bottom, ready to charm some young floozy over a big fat glass of delicately sipped wine, or maybe a brandy-bubble, a line of coke to loosen her up, I won't myself, well maybe later, I don't know how to put this but it might effect my performance, coke always making me more fascinated but ultimately disinterested; or maybe I will become some kind of sexual wild man, doing stuff I've never done before, making sinister noises, going on holiday with my long-married friends and slutty girlfriend and destabilising the other couples with our howling noises, like one of the characters in that Alan Alda film *The Four Seasons*; maybe I'll do nothing much for ages, and then, one day, I'll be walking on this hill, and I'll see somebody, and everything will turn out fine, absolutely fine.

But, frankly, I doubt it.

I sit down. On a bench.

I am at the top of a hill, on the rim of a valley, looking down towards a river, and at a road, and some flashing windshields, an Alpine cupola, an industrial estate, and beyond all this, some bluish hills, some trees, how many trees, maybe 40,000 trees, and the sky, and some clouds, which are in streaks across the sky.

Break-ups get worse as you get older – but why? Partly because relationships get more serious. As you progress through life, you're like a sports team in a tournament, each match more important than the last, the make-or-break final being the most important of all.

. . . but that's not right, is it? It's much more complex than that. So forget the tournament analogy. The way it's flawed, I suppose, is that if you lose the semi-final in a sports tournament, you can't progress to the final. But if you get dumped in the relationship that is the semi-final of your romantic life, you can still play in the final, and win.

. . . but that's not right either, is it? The analogy sucks, because relationships are not contests. You don't 'win' relationships. Human relationships, actually, are the most complex things we'll ever have to understand, and one of life's tragedies is that we're all like Saul Bellow's character Chick in his novel *Ravelstein*. We get closer to understanding human relationships as we get older, we get wiser and frailer, wiser and frailer, until the terrible moment when we achieve great wisdom, which is the same moment they wheel us into hospital on a gurney, dribbling and incontinent.

Wisdom is frailty, and vitality is ignorance, which is maybe why we prize vitality so much.

I'm forty-seven. I thought I'd understand the world by now. I thought I'd have *answers*.

But I don't.

Or do I?

Well, I know how it all started. At least I know how people *say* it all started – with the Big Bang. Thirteen billion years ago, something happened, and there was an explosion, and a tiny dot became the universe, in something like a thousandth of a second. This is the scientific explanation. We know the religious explanation – that it was God, rather than an exploding dot, and that it took a week. I would go for the scientific explanation over the religious one. But only just. To accept the scientific explanation, you have to believe, to begin with, that the entire universe was packed into this tiny dot, a dot so small that it would be dwarfed by the dot at the end of an exclamation mark. And you have to accept that this thing, known as the Singularity, burst, and the universe spewed out, and caught fire, on account of the heat generated by the energy of the explosion. The resulting fireballs were stars, one of which was the sun.

And you also have to accept that everything is made of tiny bits of electrically charged dust, and these bits of dust zoom around, and then clump together, and sometimes they stay together, on a temporary basis, because they are stronger together than they would be apart. And this clumping happens until dust clouds become planets. And then it happens *on* the planets. And on some planets, like ours, conditions are exactly right for bits of dust to clump together in more and more complex ways. Hence life. Life is really just bits of dust that clump together until they start to replicate themselves.

Given time, life is inevitable. If you got some dust, and put it in a room, and went away for ten billion years, when you got back to the room the dust would have come to life. Then if you went away for another three billion years, the dust would have invented guns and jet engines and bag-free vacuum cleaners and mortgages. After that, it's only a few more years before you get global terrorism, the internet, and Paris Hilton.

According to physicists, it takes thirteen billion years for pieces of dust to clump together into life forms intelligent enough to understand that they are, in fact, pieces of dust clumped together.

*   *   *

So the bits of dust become atoms, and the atoms form little systems, and the little systems begin to feed on the stuff around them, extracting energy from the world and breaking it down into a more disorganised form, eating and excreting, and then some of the little systems begin to make copies of themselves, or rather, I suppose, the little systems do just about everything, but it's the ones who make copies of themselves who survive – is that quite right, probably not, there's a better way of putting it, isn't there? – it's the information that survives, the information contained in the DNA of the little systems, that's the thing that survives, and over time the better ones replicate more than the less good ones, and then there's a revolution, isn't there, another big bang, and now some of the little life forms shed parts of themselves that get mixed up with parts shed by other little life forms, and for billions of years nothing happens as a result, like 'here's an arm, shall I try to mix it with, say, your leg?' and of course it doesn't work, or maybe 'here's a finger, look, I'll chop my finger off, how about mixing it with your eye, why not poke your eye out, and mix it with my finger?' and *that* doesn't work either, and over, say, a billion years, you'd try everything, wouldn't you, and one day a little part of one tiny single-celled life form mixes with another little part of another single-celled life form, these parts being gametes, and a whole new creature emerges, and when this happens trillions of times, some of these new creatures turn out to be better adapted for survival than their parents, and they pass on their tendency to reproduce in the new way, sexually that is, rather than simply by dividing into exact replicas of themselves, so now you've got sexual reproduction, which gives you different variations, and therefore evolution, and then, after you have sexual reproduction, it follows that you must have ageing and death, because the life forms that reproduce sexually and then die will have a slight advantage over those that reproduce sexually and stay around, on account of the fact that their kind will have a faster turnover, shorter generation gaps, and so they will adapt faster, evolution at first favouring short lifespans and quick adaptation, although this changes later, when life forms become more complex, when they begin to learn, but still, when you think about it, sex is the reason for death, as well as being the reason for life, which must be why we're so weird about it, treating it like some kind of god.

And, hang on, there's a law that governs lifespan, isn't there, discovered by Tom Kirkwood while he was in the bath, and the reason that the idea came to him in the bath was to do with the fact that Kirkwood's hero was Archimedes, who had solved a scientific problem in the bath; *he*'d got into the bath and noticed that, as he lowered himself into the water, the surface of the water correspondingly moved upwards, giving him a sudden insight into the nature of displacement, whereupon he jumped out of his bath, and ran into the street, naked, accosting strangers and shouting 'Eureka!' which means 'I have found it!' and this makes you wonder, doesn't it, what would happen to a scientist these days, in this cultural climate, who ran around the streets, naked, shouting 'I have found it' – he'd better have found something pretty fabulous, such as a cure for cancer, rather than simply firming up on something as rudimentary as an insight into displacement. And, anyway, Kirkwood, who wanted to emulate Archimedes – not by streaking, anybody can do *that*, but by having a ground-breaking idea – took to having long baths, and thinking about his subject while lying in the bath, his subject being why do we get old and die; and thinking about Kirkwood in his bath makes me think of Tom Wolfe, who once had a great insight into modern art while reading the Sunday edition of the *New York Times*, which he described as being exactly like a warm bath you slip into on a Sunday morning, Wolfe's insight being that, in this day and age, art has been corrupted to such an extent by its hangers-on, its demi-monde of critics and fashionistas, that artists have begun to believe their work exists primarily in a verbal realm, on the page rather than on the canvas, and thinking about *this* makes me think about breakthroughs in general, the moments that people have discovered something – Parkinson with his Law that work expands to fit the time you've got, Peter with his Principle that executives get promoted to their level of incompetence, Einstein with his insight that mass, everything in other words, is really just information about energy, Darwin with his study of the beaks of finches and the necks of tortoises, when he had his breakthrough it terrified him, this notion that there is no plan, no higher authority, no God, no greater good, no humanity as such, but just infinitesimally changing gradations through the years, just the illusion of humanity, the illusion of progress, it terrified him that the whole of life, therefore, is essentially meaningless, that we are, as John Grey would say more than a century later, 'currents in the drift of genes'; in any case I wish I could have a breakthrough, I wish I could have a moment of clear thought, it's been appalling, five hundred days of mental attrition, my mind gone, my thoughts a mess, every morning hoping that today might be the day, sitting there at my computer, and then moving to the sofa, and suddenly it's lunchtime, my spirits beginning their daily descent.

Which reminds me of the thing they say on planes. I was on a plane just before my relationship ended, five months ago now; I'd flown to Geneva to meet my old friend Robin, who was working on the particle accelerator in CERN, where they split atoms and smash tiny bits of dust into each other at almost the speed of light. Robin was working on the essential problem in physics – namely, why do tiny things clump together, in other words why do we exist and what are we doing? Of course nobody knows, nobody has any idea, but he had apparently devised an elaborate set of mirrors to capture the flight of photons, particles of light – so I went to see him, I hadn't seen him for twenty-three years, and when I got off the plane I went to bed and woke up with an appalling headache, it was the worst headache I'd had in my life, and I called Robin, but he did not answer, and I called him again, but he did not answer, he never answered, and I went to look for an aspirin, and as I was walking along I stopped by the side of a road, and a car drew up, a sports car, and I remembered Robin had been a sports car man, and the man inside the sports car looked very familiar, he was waving at me, beckoning me, so I went to the car, and the man opened the door, and I got in the car, and the man looked exactly like Robin, but I could see there was something strange about the man, and then I realised the strange thing was that the man was not Robin, just someone who looked exactly like Robin had looked twenty-three years earlier, I realised he'd look quite different now, he would be forty-five or forty-six, and the reason he was not answering his phone was that he had been rushed to hospital; while I was sitting in the car, looking at the young man, his forty-five- or forty-six-year-old body was being operated on.

And on the way back, the stewardess's voice came over the tannoy. 'We are beginning our descent,' she said. I thought that was a pretty good way to describe the situation in general – my headache, my stomach ache, the fact that I wasn't sleeping well, my strange psychological symptoms, my inability to think straight, and my creeping paranoia about everything, for instance what really happened on 9/11, and why is capitalism spinning out of control, and how come we are ruining the planet, me included, and not doing anything about it, and also why, when we can have anything we want, are we less happy than ever, and why are people so bad-mannered, and why does racism persist, why is dog food so scandalously unhealthy, why does nobody trust each other any more, to the extent that even our marmalade and mayonnaise jars have plastic seals in case somebody wants to put poison in the jar and demand a ransom, a sensible precaution, because it happens, it definitely happens, it's something to do with information, maybe that's the key to everything, terrorism being a product of information, but why then, when we all saw the mayhem caused by the Washington sniper, why does bin Laden not do a similar thing, a sniper in every town, or maybe bring one town to its knees, completely close it down, close down the schools, the factories, just one shooting a day, it would be cheap, it's not as if there aren't enough terrorists willing to do it, and it would be much more effective than a bomb, a bomb with its classic narrative, the shock and horror followed by the media aftermath, the deployment of troops, the strange emerging details. Well, I'll tell you why bin Laden does not let snipers loose, it's because it's not really him that's behind it all, it's us of course, it was us all along, our undercover people infiltrating their undercover people and encouraging them to do all sorts of stuff, and they thought it suited them, but really it suited us, these heinous acts emerging, a sort of evolution, everybody on a need-to-know basis, Rumsfeld and Cheney not-quite-knowing, aspiring to and developing a higher ignorance, an ability to know and yet not know – Elizabeth Wurtzel writes about this in herself – I think it might be the ultimate human ability, as you get older you find yourself knowing-and-not-knowing more and more things, as you plough on, towards the inevitable end, at first denying small things and then more and more, that's what I was thinking on the plane, we are beginning our descent . . . well said, I thought, tipping back another small bottle of wine, I was drinking back then, I was mentally unravelling, it was just before I was dumped, I came back, and we had some people round for lunch the next day, and I was of course in denial about my drinking, I accept that now, and we were getting things ready, it was the first warm Sunday, we were eating on the terrace, and we had no wine, I mentioned the fact that we had no wine, and of course this did not matter, but I made a point of getting a bottle of fortified wine, I think port, out of the cupboard, port that was normally used for cooking, and I poured myself a glass as we got everything ready, and it was a big glass, and the mother of my little boy went outside to sit down, and I took the glass and tipped it back, poured the whole lot down my throat, an instinctive gesture, and this was the exact moment she chose to come back into the kitchen, having forgotten something, possibly the salt, and she looked at me, and I said, 'I'll stop drinking', and I did, but it was too late, she saw me, I'd cut down considerably, was not a drunk, but still, that look of disappointment was enough to make me stop completely, too late of course, too late, too late, when you get to a certain age you realise that, sometimes, it's just too late, and this is what I'm thinking as I get off the bench and walk along the path towards my little boy and the mother of my little boy, feeling anxious now, anger welling up in my stomach, I'm sweating now, the fever still a presence, as it has been for weeks, I am hot and damp, my hair a seeping rug, my face red, my head aching, my thoughts starting to veer out of control, the cartilage in my knee hurting as I hit the sloping ground. It's too late. This is what I'm thinking as I see the first signs of houses on the other side of the hill, in another minute or two I'll be able to see the house I used to sort of live in with my little boy and the mother of my little boy, but it's too late; this is what I'm thinking.

Chapter 4

I ran into her at a station.
 I was with my father.

I hadn't seen her in a long time.
 She wrote her phone number on a piece of paper, but it fell on the ground, and she bent to pick it up, and I ruffled her hair with my hand.
 Afterwards, my father said, 'You ruffled her hair.'

I knew it would work out.

The beginning was good. But the bit after the beginning was also good. That's when you know you're on to a winner.

This is what I'm thinking as I walk down the hill, trying to keep calm, trying to think in an orderly fashion; I'm thinking about the start, and when we first went on holiday, and I'm thinking about the first time we played crazy golf, and I'm thinking about the car, how I'll see the car very soon, and my mind is focused on the car, how it will make me feel, she will be packing the car, things will be folded, she will be packing the car, and I will walk past the car, trying to keep calm, but this is fine, because I do not have to face this yet, I still have to walk through the woods, but even as I think this I realise I will soon be in an area where I recognise every tree, where trees are no longer just trees, but these trees, these particular trees, and this the place where I dumped the leaves, these particular leaves.

To get back to the crazy golf: we were perfectly matched. Nothing between us in terms of points. She was more consistent in her putting. I would go to pieces, sometimes taking four or five extra shots, but then I would make up for it with a run of good shots.

Part of me thinks that I might walk up to the drive and walk past the car and go into the house and my little boy will run up to me and I will bend down and he will hug me, my little boy, and his mother will say something, she will say I know things have been difficult, something like that, but anyway why not come along, why not come on holiday with us, why not do that, but this is only part of me that thinks this, and the other part of me knows this will not happen.

But if the universe is infinite, and everything is clumping together and falling apart in the blink of an eye, and time does not exist, then there is a world where this is happening, where she is saying these things, but I will not allow myself to dwell on the matter.

I am now walking past the place where they found the skeletons, and I remember the excitement when they found the skeletons, first a skull, then another skull, the skulls having been separated from the skeletons, which were in a shallow grave, hands tied behind their backs. The bones were brown but otherwise well preserved. I saw them in the soil. They were the bones of

142

medieval soldiers who had been captured and beheaded. Then their heads had been thrown down the hill. The skulls appear every few years. Walkers find them and call the police, thinking something terrible has happened.

The beginning was good, and the bit after the beginning was good, everything was fine for a year, and then I ran out of money, and then she knew something about me she hadn't known before. We sat down and I had to explain the concept of no money, no money at all and no access to money, I had to explain the concept of having no money at the age of forty-four, and she asked me why I had no money and I shook my head and put my elbows on the table and balanced my chin on my hands. It was a good question.

A few days before this I had been standing at the back of a line at a post office, holding a carrier bag full of pennies.

I was carrying a ball of metal, a heavy ball of metal.

I was sweating.

I was carrying a bag full of pennies, and I was forty-four years old.

I stood at the end of the line, trying to muster dignity. Everybody else in the line, I thought, had more dignity than me. Some of these people were here to send parcels, and they wanted to know how fast the parcels could be sent.

But I had a bag of pennies. I kept thinking: at least nobody knows what's in my bag. But then it would chink. And there was something about the way I was holding it. And then there was the matter of what I'd say to the person behind the screen.

Why does a forty-four-year-old man stand in a line at a post office with a bag of pennies? He does it because he is desperate. I had spent my overdraft. I had no savings account. I had borrowed from every person that might have lent me money.

I had scoured my flat for banknotes. Then I had emptied all my jars, and taken the silver.

And now I was down to the pennies. I had about a thousand.

That was three years ago, almost to the day. It was the week our little boy was conceived.

Our relationship was in the balance.

Teetering.

We still lived in different towns.

I knew she suspected that I might have financial problems.

I knew she worried that these problems were part of a greater problem.

I knew I didn't have enough money to pay for my rail ticket in a week's time. But I had a plan, and I was sure it would work.

For the moment, I just had to get through the next few days.

When I got to the counter, I held up the bag. Of course, the person behind the screen did not see the significance of the bag. I put my hand in, and took out a handful of coins. They were that terrible colour – the loser's colour.

The woman shook her head. She would not change my coins into notes, or even into silver. But she said the local bank might provide the service.

I trudged out, and turned down the hill, and sometimes, when I look back at myself, I think: *there*, that's the moment.

That's the moment I became middle-aged.

I had often run out of money. Sometimes I had money, and sometimes not. When I was younger, this was fine. It was fine that I was the sort of person who was sometimes rich and sometimes poor. And now, for some reason, it was not fine. Now, I was too old not to have money, in the same way that I was too old to sleep on floors or to arrive somewhere without having booked a hotel; I was too old to have messy hair or to be unshaven or to wear ripped jeans. Life was closing in, that's what I felt, as I walked down the street with my bag of money, the heavy bag of money I was carrying because I did not have any money.

But what is money anyway? This is what I'm thinking now, as I inch down the hill, walking sideways, cartilage pinching at my knee. Where does money come from? I know this, somewhere at the back of my mind. It's banks, isn't it? Banks create money by lending it to people. That doesn't sound right, does it? But it's true. Say I'm a bank, and I lend you some money. Well, that's money I haven't got, isn't it? But if I lend it to you, it's money you owe me, plus interest. By lending it to you, I have created it from nothing. Hold on a moment. How can I lend money I don't have? Easy. I can do it because I'm a bank. That's the whole point of banks. That's what banking is all about, lending money you don't have, and then collecting interest. This is our system. This is the capitalist system. It's what we vote for. It's why we go to war. When someone describes us as 'freedom-loving people', that's the freedom they are talking about. They are talking about the freedom to create money out of nothing. It looked like a good system, at the beginning. It looked like a good system for a while. But now it's getting old, the system of creating money out of nothing. Now it's on its last legs.

Nobody really knows when it started; like most things, it *emerged*. It emerged three hundred-odd years ago, in the days of gold coins and local goldsmiths who kept their valuables in vaults, and at some point began to rent space in their vaults to people who wanted to store *their* valuables, the goldsmiths giving these people receipts, which began to have their own transferable value, becoming the first rudimentary banknotes.

145

And then the penny must have dropped. Somebody, nobody knows who, but almost certainly a seventeenth-century English goldsmith, had a Eureka moment: *I've got all this gold! And people don't need it now they're using the receipts! It's not mine, but . . . it might as well be!*

Naturally, this was a secret Eureka moment. He did not rush out into the streets and *tell* people about his idea, even though it was very, very good. How good was it? It was one of the best ideas anybody has ever had.

Why not pretend to have more valuables than you actually have?

But pretty soon somebody must have found out what the goldsmiths were doing. They were printing more banknotes than they were entitled to, creating money from nothing, and somebody must have noticed. Maybe they were wearing furs or gold chains. I'm thinking of the scene in *Goodfellas*, after the robbery, when the criminals have a party, and turn up in flash new cars and furs, and Robert De Niro, the boss, says, 'What did I tell you? What did I tell you? What did I tell you? You don't buy anything, you hear me? Don't buy anything!' The goldsmiths must have been like Nicky Eyes and Frankie the Wop, or whoever, walking around in finery, because people, the people who had stashed their valuables in the goldsmiths' vaults, worked out what the goldsmiths were doing, and threatened them. The goldsmiths had been rumbled. But this did not stop them. Their solution was to give their accusers a percentage of the profits. They cut them in.

And that was the birth of the *interest-rate spread*. The goldsmith would pay a small amount of interest to the depositor, and charge a larger amount of interest to borrowers. And who were these borrowers? People who needed a lot of money. People, for instance, who wanted to fight wars, or start empires, or sail wooden ships thousands of miles across the world to plunder another person's resources – or else sink the ships of another plunderer. I'm thinking of ships pulling up alongside each other, firing broadsides, tons of metal smashing through wood, clouds of cordite hanging in the air, men being torn apart by cannon fire, the gun crews in the hold, the officers walking around on the deck, affecting composure. That's what people did when they borrowed money.

The biggest borrower was the British government. They needed £1.2 million to fight the French. That's why the Bank of England was set up. The year: 1694.

So what do you do if you're a bank? You create money by lending it to people. But when you create money, you change the world. When you create money, there is more money in the world, even though there is not more wealth. You have not made the world more valuable. You have not created more food, or more shelter, or more happiness, or more love. Actually, you have taken away happiness. You have taken away love.

What you have done is this: you have increased the money supply. That's one thing you've done. You have also increased the proportion of the money supply that you own. That's another thing you've done.

Say you lend money to a businessman. That's money you have created. Before you lent the money, it did not exist. Now it does. The businessman uses the money to advertise, so that he can get ahead of his rivals. Pretty soon, his rivals will need to advertise, too. So you lend them money. And now everybody is back to square one. Everybody is equal again. But now there is more money in circulation. And everybody owes you interest. And because everybody owes you interest, they have to work harder. They have to run in order to stay still. They have to exploit new markets.

Still, you are the bank. Nobody expected you to be a saint. You have made everybody work harder, certainly, by increasing the money supply without increasing any resources, and now you own a bigger proportion of the world, and you have set people against each other, rather like the Americans in the Reagan administration who sold weapons to both sides in the Iran/Iraq war, selling the Iranians long-range bombers, and then selling the Iraqis anti-aircraft guns to shoot down the bombers.

So you think you are sitting pretty, don't you? But you're not sitting pretty. Because, now that you own more of the world, it's a less valuable world, isn't it? Now that everybody spends a not inconsiderable part of their time working out how to pay you back the interest on their loans, their businesses work less well. Some of them might go bust. But you don't want that, do you? Empty factories are no good to you. Businesses that go bust are no good to you.

You are caught in a vicious spiral. You can't stop adding to the money supply, because, if you do, people will go bust, and the economy will grind to a halt. So what can you do? You can carry on creating money out of nothing. That's the only thing you can do. You can't un-create the money you have already created. And you can't stop creating it, because people will go bust. So you have to carry on pumping money into the system. This is called economic growth.

You are a bank. And my question is: are you beginning to have an existential crisis? Are you feeling the pinch, somewhere in your soul? Is it just a little bit undignified, the fact that you have to send people credit card applications all the time? And all those emails? And the TV ads, with celebrities doing your begging for you? Does this not feel undignified?

And lots of weird things are happening now, aren't they? Frogs are not yet falling from the sky, I grant you that. But give them time, the frogs. Give them time. All the same, weird stuff is happening. When you lend money, have you thought about who you are lending it to? I have. You are lending it to people who are good at exploiting other people. You are lending it to people who have come up with a good angle for making a quick return on your money. You are lending it to people who can find and exploit new markets. You are lending it to people who can create needs in the consumer. You are lending it to people who can make other people feel empty and anxious. You are creating a world in your own image. You are exploiting people; it is only natural that they will need to exploit others. Abuse trickles down. Mistakes beget mistakes. Because, as you must realise by now, this whole enterprise was a mistake, wasn't it?

How does it feel, when people come to you and tell you about their schemes? Are you becoming glutted with people's wicked ingenuity? Oh, the gambling schemes, the pornographic schemes. The advertising. And advertising, as we have seen, begets advertising. So the very nature of advertising changes over time, doesn't it, as everybody begins to do it, getting more subtly malicious, not just telling people what the product is like, but making them feel bad about themselves if they don't have the product. And then advertising seeps into everything, doesn't it, creating a general sense of malaise and anxiety. And now if you pick up a magazine it's no longer a vector of information, not in the way it used to be before the seepage of advertising. It's not, primarily speaking, about selling information to the reader. No, now it's about selling the reader to the advertiser, and thus corrupting the flow of information, not only creating a world of anxiety – a world in which people do not like their bodies, do not feel sexy, do not feel cool, but flip through magazines, feeling half-dead because they don't have this car or that piece of furniture – but something worse still, a world in which people do not trust the most basic source of information. Because it's there to support the advertising, isn't it?

If you increase the money supply and charge people interest, you make people nastier! That's the main effect of your actions! You increase the gap between those who exploit others, such as advertisers, and pornographers, and people who run gambling websites, and, and, on the other hand, people who do not exploit others, such as nurses and me . . . me, I suppose, with my words. You are making harmless people poorer, and nasty people, comparatively speaking, richer. Do you not know this? Do you not know that this is the reason for the death of love?

Ah, but it's a Faustian pact, isn't it, an undignified Faustian pact, it's not as if it's any fun for you, stuffing envelopes with credit offers and sending spam emails through the post, not exactly glamorous, is it?

And the frogs will fall from the sky!

And people are getting ruder, aren't they, less well mannered, and you must see that, pushing each other out of the way, it's happening to me even, I'm just as bad as the rest of them. There I was a few weeks ago, just before I was dumped, pushing my little boy along in a pram, and I almost mowed a guy down, and when challenged by the mother of my little boy about my rudeness, my total disregard for another human being, I said, 'Well, he should have seen me coming!'

She said, correctly: 'He was blind.'

Are we not all more anxious, more aggressive, more prone to depression? I keep trying to explain this to my parents, but they don't get it, and all I can say is that in their day it was still possible to be a nice person and have a big house and a new car and not be in debt, but these days you can't do that without selling your soul, these days you have to be actively encouraging people to spend money, rather than, say, teaching them history or something.

The banks own us. We're all in debt. There's not enough money to go around, because of the interest-rate spread. But the banks don't want to put everybody out of business. So they are forced to increase the money supply by lending more money, thus making the problem worse. And they can't stop. And it's taking a terrible toll on our society. It's encouraging people to be nastier. It's encouraging people to be more exploitative. More people are going over to the dark side. There is a wider gulf, financially, between exploiters and non-exploiters. Cooperation between groups of people is becoming less and less worthwhile, because, now that everybody owes interest to the banks, sharing will always produce a shortfall. Exploitation is the only way forward.

As soon as you start increasing the money supply – as happened in, say, 1650 – the end is in sight. Certain things are guaranteed to happen. Marketing will become predatory. Advertising will become ubiquitous. Corporations will need to spend an increasing proportion of their budgets getting people to want things, and a decreasing proportion of their budgets actually making things. The growth area: making people unhappy. That's progress. That's what progress is. It's all about finding ways of making people unhappy. Progress is just one big unhappiness machine.

In the future, everybody will work harder, in order to stand still. People's standards will change all the time. An ordinary toaster used to look fine, but now you are judged by your toaster. There used to be ten types of cooker. Now there are ten thousand. There used to be posh clothes and casual clothes. Now there is a ladder with fifty rungs, and every rung on the ladder is a recognisable badge of status.

Everything is a commodity. Just look at, God, I don't know, anything. Like body hair. Women used to shave their legs and armpits and pluck their eyebrows and get their hair cut. Now they wax their legs and shave their armpits and trim their pubic hair and wax their pubic hair and dye their eyelashes and tint their hair simultaneously with several colours and supplement it with hair extensions, and every new activity requires tools and materials, such as trimming devices and depilatory creams and laser hair-removal machines. Now men are waxing their chests, and soon they'll be shaping and trimming their pubic hair. It's economic growth. It's unstoppable.

And now retailers are hiring experts to advise them on how to sell more stuff, experts who cheerfully tell us that, if it wasn't for impulse purchasing, if it wasn't for people buying stuff that they don't strictly need, or even want, 'the economy would collapse'. And what do these experts, these gurus, do? They tell shops how to arrange items on shelves, so that people will be diverted on the way to buying what they need towards something they might suddenly want. They understand the science of peripheral vision, the placing of baskets, the intricacies of 'pester power', getting kids to want more, and the devilish art of designing shelves to be more eye-catching. And once one retail chain hires a guru, everybody else needs to hire a guru, too. So everybody will be back to square one again. They'll just have to borrow more money, won't they?

And one day, you'll be on a golf course, and you'll hit a ball down a hole, and you'll bend down to pick the ball out of the hole, and there, in the hole, will be an ad. And another day, you will be standing in a urinal. And you'll be pissing on an ad.

So it all started with people going out in boats to plunder the world, and borrowing money, and here we are, unable to escape ads, here we are, new products growing into every space available, like cancers, getting everywhere, strangling us, using up exponentially more of the world's resources, I heard about a new type of sugar the other day, a better type of sugar, a brand that's several times more expensive, and I thought, *it's happening to sugar! Is nothing sacred?* And the answer, of course, is no, nothing is sacred, and for some reason I thought of the world of feminine hygiene, is that what it's called, sanitary protection, or whatever, and how it used to be based on five days every month, but now it's more, with all these pads available, pads to make women feel 'fresh' on normal days, the implication being that they would not be fresh otherwise, and now the market is growing towards its end point of twenty-eight days per month, every day accounted for, causing a global toll of thousands of square miles of forest clearance, cotton production, pesticide factories and transatlantic shipping lines, cardboard packaging, ink factories, and offices full of designers, advertisers and marketers, most of whom drive to work in SUVs and borrow vast amounts of money to finance their own discerning purchases.

And three hundred years ago, when people were sailing away from their European bases to plunder the world, the English and the French and the Spanish and the Dutch, vying with each other, as it turned out, to see who would be the main beneficiaries of the coming industrial society (it was the English), somebody had another bright idea, the idea of selling guns to an African tribe, which immediately meant that all the other tribes needed guns, too, either that or face certain extinction, and what did the African tribes have that we wanted? Only one thing, it turned out – people for use as slaves. So economic growth caused slavery, and slavery, of course, caused the sort of racism that's impossible to eradicate, even now, hundreds of years later, not simple racism, negative feelings towards somebody other than yourself, but complex racism, based on humiliation and shame, when one group of people feels vulnerable, believes that another group of people despises them, and this rift never really heals: if you leave it alone, it gets worse, and if you intervene, with affirmative action schemes, it also gets worse.

That's what happens when you increase the money supply and charge interest and keep on pumping money in – you cause exploitation and tribalism and the death of community; everybody becomes an individual economic unit, gulling and tricking everybody else out of their money, and now we all have to work twice as hard, typically both members of a couple, tired and weary with guilt and self-loathing when we arrive home in the evenings, and yet full of expectation, wanting the better life, having seen tens of thousands of ads, expecting to be happy and sexy and glamorous, but feeling like debtors, financially and spiritually, overdrawn at every bank you care to name, coming

154

home to the death of love and the death of hope, and exploiting everybody in sight, and hating ourselves, and getting up in the morning and doing it all over again, sucking resources from the earth, and when will it all end? Sooner than we think, I suppose. Sooner than we think, and all because of money.

And money was exactly what I did not have three years ago, which was precisely why I was carrying a heavy bag of pennies to the bank.

I think: there: that's the moment.

That's the moment I became middle-aged.

I went into the bank. The guy at the counter was young. I asked him if he could change the coins into notes. He didn't see why not. But he'd have to check. He checked with an older guy. The older guy was younger than me. I got one note and five or six coins. That would have to last me for a few days.

Then came the day I had planned to visit my girlfriend.

My plan was simple. Walk to the station. And then buy my ticket with my dud card. I'd done it before. The machines at the station, I thought, didn't have the capacity to tell dud cards from good ones. I was sure of this.

I was wrong.

My train would in five minutes.

And my girlfriend would be waiting for me at the other end.

Like I said – the relationship was in the balance.

At forty-four, you do not have the option of cancelling your weekend date at the last minute because you're too broke to buy a train ticket.

I had to catch the train.

I did not have a penny. Not a penny.

I had no ticket. So I could not walk on to the train.

My only option was to run.

*   *   *

So I started to run, a minute before the train was due to leave the station. Having no ticket, I could not get through the automatic barriers. I would have to aim at the manned section of the barrier, the bit for people with bags that will not fit through the automatic barriers. I would have to run at the barrier, and get through, and on the train, without being stopped by the man at the barrier. I would have to give the impression, to the man at the barrier, that I had a ticket, and was bursting through the barrier for reasons of convenience. This is what I was thinking as I ran through the station. Past the snackpoints and coffee concessions. Past the people who are trying to snag you on your way to the train. These people did not exist twenty years ago, did they? These people are here because of economic growth.

Past the place selling coffee and doughnuts. Past a place selling Japanese food. Past the people marketing a new type of car. Past the people handing out free samples of chocolate, to hook you on to another brand. Past the place selling expensive cheeses, and the place selling cheap food at marked-up prices. Past the betting shop and the wine bar and the newsagents, where the Indian guy always asks you, when you buy a newspaper, if you also want to buy a ton of fancy chocolate at reduced prices.

Running past all these things, my ankle beginning to hurt. Running past all these things, and the people, too, slaloming between the people, aged forty-four, picking up speed, my lungs beginning to hurt, the years of abusing my lungs having taken their toll, snot-shoe alveoli being worked to capacity, heartbeat rapidly rising, spiky balls slamming against the sides of my arteries, my face reddening, thinking that I would have to give the impression of being a man in a hurry, a man who might decide to burst through the manned part of the barrier as part of

156

an honest arrangement, trying to look like a man who might burst through a barrier honestly, an above-board burster.

Accelerating towards the barrier. Lungs at full capacity. Ankle holding out, but only just.

A final burst of acceleration, as the man on the platform prepares to blow the whistle.

Approaching the barrier, which is manned by a black guy in uniform. A black guy, younger than me, in uniform. Looking into the black guy's eyes. An instinctive grasping at my pocket, as if groping for a ticket to show him.

I said something: 'Is this the Eastbourne train?'

Something like that.

This was the moment of bursting.

I looked into his eyes, groped for my imaginary ticket, a lie of sorts, a total lie in fact, and then I burst, our bodies touching at the barrier, and then I asked him a question about the train, to distract him from the question he might have asked me, the question I dreaded, and he did not ask me the question I dreaded, but looked at me, and said something, and I ran on, beyond him, away from his sphere of influence, and he watched me as I ran away from him, and I had done enough, just enough, I was through, he would not want to make a fuss now, and the man on the platform was about to blow the whistle, and I stepped on the train, and the man on the platform blew the whistle, and the automatic doors closed, and the train moved out of the station, and I was on the train without a ticket, and without any means of buying a ticket, and there would be a man checking tickets on the train, but I had a plan, and I thought it might work.

On the train I thought about the man who would ask me for my ticket, and I thought about the arrangements we had made for the upcoming few days, and I thought about the books I had given my girlfriend, my six favourite books.

That evening, we were going to the cinema to see *The Village*, a movie directed by M. Night Shyamalan. The cinema, I realised, would not now accept my card.

The next day, we were going to a party in someone's garden.

Another thing we had planned was a visit to HMS *Victory*, the ship on which Nelson died in the heat of the Battle of Trafalgar, his greatest victory. My girlfriend liked Nelson. He was everything I was not. He was like the Tom Hanks character in *Saving Private Ryan*. He knew exactly what to do in a situation, and then he did it, with minimum fuss. Every man that served under him understood this, and practically worshipped him because of it. Nelson made the seas safe for British ships. If there was one man who won his country the right to the spoils of the Industrial Revolution, it was him.

What a guy. When he was wounded, he ignored the pain and the misery with an almost ostentatious show of calm. In 1794, at the age of thirty-six, he was standing near a British gun emplacement in Corsica, when a cannonball exploded near by. Nelson's face was peppered with gravel, splinters and sand, and these things hit him with such force that he was virtually blinded in the right eye. The skin was ripped from his forehead and scalp, producing a huge amount of blood. He was knocked to the ground by the blast of an explosion. His head was cut to shreds. Rocks had been driven into his eye socket. His reaction: 'Except for a very slight scratch towards my right eye . . . I have received no hurt whatsoever.'

Three years later, Nelson, by now a rear-admiral, was attempting to board a Spanish ship in Tenerife, when he was shot just above the elbow. A contemporary account describes it as a horrifyingly bloody moment; a lump of hot lead severed the artery in his right arm. More or less immediately, he explained to the men around him everything they needed to know: that a tourniquet would have to be applied to his arm (he used his silk scarf), that his arm would have to be amputated, because it was beyond redemption, and that he wanted to have the operation immediately. He would need to get in a small rowing boat, and go across the harbour to another ship, where he knew there was a surgeon. When he got to the ship, somebody offered to help him up the rope ladder, whereupon he said, 'No, I have yet my legs and one arm.' Have you ever seen one of these ships? To arrive on the deck, you have to clamber from your bobbing boat to the rope ladder, and then haul yourself upwards for about thirty feet. To make things worse, the ship is moving, and the sides of it bow outwards, so for a while you're climbing outwards as well as upwards. When Nelson arrived on deck, the officers saluted him, taking off their hats. He took off his own hat in reply, using his left hand, as if he was going about his daily business. Which he was, in a way, the business on this particular day being the swift arrangement of the removal of his right arm. Two days later, he was learning to write with his left hand.

On the train, while I waited for the man to challenge me about my ticket, I thought of Nelson, and of Nelson's wounds, and of the fact that we had planned a trip to HMS *Victory*, to stand on the spot where Nelson died. And I thought about the books I had given her, my six favourite books. The books I had given her were: *Independence Day*, by Richard Ford, *Rabbit at Rest*, by John Updike, *Seize the Day*, by Saul Bellow, *The Bonfire of the Vanities*, by Tom Wolfe, *Money*, by Martin Amis, and *Mailman*, by J. Robert Lennon.

They were all books about middle-aged failures and losers. They were about weak, middle-aged losers who had dribbled their lives away. I wondered if she'd been reading them, these books about middle-aged losers.

My plan was to walk up the train, to see where the ticket collector was, and then to move to the other end of the train, and hope that, by the time he arrived in my carriage, I would have reached my stop, and then, after that, my plan was to walk straight through the manned barrier, and then, after that, my plan was to get into my girlfriend's car, and either explain, immediately, that I had no money, or wait a while, and play the situation by ear. One thing I could do, I realised, was locate the ticket collector, and move away from him, down the train, and then, when the train stopped at a station, get out of the train, and run along the train, re-entering the train behind him.

The train pulled out of the city and picked up speed. I was sweating and panting. I had pulled muscles. My knee ached. My shoulder ached. I sat down, and then stood up. I walked along the train. No sign of a ticket collector.

In *Independence Day*, Frank Bascombe, a divorced man in his forties, describes a week during his mid-life crisis; against a backdrop of angst and dithering, he drives to his ex-wife's house, picks up his son and takes his son to the Baseball Hall of Fame, where the son has an accident, and Bascombe then tries not to fall apart, and almost succeeds, but ends up humiliated and broken.

In *Rabbit at Rest*, Harry Angstrom, a recently retired car sales-man, takes his granddaughter on a sailing trip. Against a back-drop of angst and dithering, he has a heart attack, and tries not to fall apart, but does, ending up on his deathbed, humiliated and broken.

*   *   *

160

In *Seize the Day*, Tommy Wilhelm, a failed actor, tries to borrow money from his father to pay his child support. The father refuses. Against a backdrop of angst and dithering, Wilhelm decides to invest everything he has on the stock market, and goes bust, ending up humiliated and broken.

In *The Bonfire of the Vanities*, Sherman McCoy, a married investment banker, goes on a date with his mistress, and, driving into a poor part of town, hits a young black guy and flees the scene. Against a backdrop of angst and dithering, we watch as his investments go sour and the cops close in; in the end, he is dragged off to prison, humiliated and broken.

In *Money*, John Self, a would-be film producer, attempts to make a film, but loses the plot, and, against a backdrop of angst and dithering, and also overeating and boozing, and also taking drugs, falls apart, ending up broken, humiliated and suicidal.

In *Mailman*, Albert Lipincott, a pathetic, middle-aged failure, arrives at the end of his tether, and falls apart. Thinking he is dying, he wanders around, trying to talk to the few acquaintances and family members who will listen, but he alienates everybody; at one point, he is ejected from a public library for masturbating. At the start of the book, he is *already* broken and humiliated, and from that point, he spirals ever downwards.

These were the six books I had given her. They were my favourite books, I said, and I gave a reason for this, and the reason was that I identified with the characters.

The ticket inspector got on the train after half an hour. I watched him from the end of the carriage as he moved towards me, checking tickets. He was a clipper and a scribbler. Good

161

news: inspectors who clip chads and mark tickets in ballpoint pen take twice as long as inspectors who merely scan tickets, or those who will accept a ticket waved at them from a distance. I once travelled on a train in which a ticket collector moved up the train, selling tickets to those who had not already bought them, and then got off. After this, another ticket collector got on, and told us that all the tickets we had just bought were invalid, and we'd have to buy them all over again. Later, at the terminal station, it was explained to me that the first ticket collector had been a 'phantom' – a guy who had been fired, but kept the uniform, and also some out-of-date ticketing equipment, enough to fool punters. I was told that, at any one time, several of these guys were on the loose, moving up and down the country, using their expert knowledge of timetables and ticketing protocol.

I watched the ticket inspector move up the train. I moved from carriage to carriage. He was pushing me towards the front of the train. It was going to be close. It was close. But I was lucky. When the train pulled into my station, he was in my carriage. He was feet away. And then the automatic doors opened, and I stepped on to the platform.

It was a hot late afternoon. I was sweaty and anxious. I was twitchy. I walked through the barrier unchallenged. She was waiting in the car. I got in. We pulled away from the station. And then we had a short conversation about the books. She had read *Independence Day*.

She said, 'Frank Bascombe. You told me you liked him.'

'I don't *like* him . . .'

'You said you identify with him.'

'Not . . . as such.'

'Do you really identify with him? He's a weak, watery sort of

162

man. He doesn't have any clue what he's doing. He doesn't even know what he wants out of life.'

'Well, does anybody?'

'What do you mean? Of course they do.'

She drove. I should have opened the window and let the wind blow my hair. I really should have done that.

I thought of the other characters. Pretty soon, she would come to the other characters. Sad, slipping Tommy Wilhelm, with his pockets full of pills and cigarette butts. John Self – did he have any saving graces? No, he did not. He was weak, a liar and a fool. He loved pornography, drugs and fast food. He was one of the sleaziest characters in modern fiction.

Jesus, I thought. Harry Angstrom – a fat, lazy, guzzling idiot. Sherman McCoy – an adulterous crook. Albert Lipincott – masturbating in public. Masturbating in public as a cry for help.

Fucking Bascombe, I thought. Bascombe was the best of them. Bascombe was the best by far.

We got back. She backed into the drive. Then we were sitting at the kitchen table.

I said: 'You know what? We don't *have* to see the film.'

'But you wanted to see the film.'

'I do. But I was just saying. We don't *have* to.'

'But . . . I want to see the film.'

Later, I had a thought.

I said, 'It's at the Picture House, right? And I don't think . . . I have an *idea* they don't take cards at the Picture House.'

'Of course they take cards.'

'Which would be fine, except for I had some trouble with mine. The stripe's down, I think. The magnetic stripe. But in any case, I'm not sure they take cards. I'm sure I was in a situation where . . . or maybe it wasn't me. I think it was more like I heard

something, it's obviously nothing, I'm probably confusing it
with something else.'

And then:

'No, I'm just remembering this now, it wasn't the Picture
House, or at least I don't think so, it will come to me.'

And:

'But, you know, just in case – do you have cash? In case my
memory is not faulty about this Picture House thing?'

And:

'And I think my stripe's down.'

And:

'Nice tea, by the way.'

And later:

'It's not that I don't have any money. It's more that, it's a time
thing, a payment thing, and it's my fault really, my slackness
with invoicing, because . . .'

And later still:

'The thing is, I was never a drug *addict*. For a time, I had a
habit. And now I don't. Now I can take it or leave it. And in fact,
I choose to leave it. It's like my drinking. Remember when you
met me – I drank your drinks cabinet, right? In two days! That's
how long it took me. Back then, I had a drink problem. Now, I
don't.'

And then:

'It feels really good, you know, getting all this off my chest.'

* * *

And:

'You're not, I mean I hope you're not upset, like upset in a major way, like in a really major way.'

And:

'Shall we still go and see the film?'

Outside it had started to rain. We got in the car and drove to the Picture House through the rainy streets. This could go either way, I was thinking. We parked. She paid. The film was weird. I could not decide if it was weird in a good way or weird in a bad way. Later, people would say it was a clear demonstration that M. Night Shyamalan, who both wrote and directed it, was having some kind of terrible crisis. It's about a community in what appears to be nineteenth-century New England. They are like Amish people. Every so often, somebody will say something about 'Those of whom we do not speak' – evil spirits that roam the land. Sometimes you catch glimpses of these devils – they wear red cloaks and look really scary. All the young people are so scared of the evil spirits that they don't dare to leave the village. In the end, you find out that this is all happening now, in modern America – the adults are hippy refuseniks, trying to protect their children from the modern world. They take it in turns to wear the cloak and scare people.

It was weird in a good way, I decided.

The next day we went to the garden party. It was a bright, sunny afternoon. Somebody asked me what I did. I once saw a French film, *Le Parfum de Sophie*, in which the hero, a handsome drifter, is at some kind of garden party, and someone asks him what he does, and he says, '*Rien.*' It's a great moment. Imagine being able to say that! From the moment I saw the film, that was one of my ambitions – to be at a garden party, and, when somebody asks me what I do, to say, 'Nothing.'

'What do you do?'

'Oh, I'm sort of trying to write a book.'

'What's it about?'

'It's about being fat.'

'Oh.'

'Yes. It's about being fat.'

'Oh.'

We were standing on the lawn, and somebody approached with some glasses of wine on a tray, and I said, 'Make sure I only have one of these. At most, two. Because if I have more than two, that's it. There's no stopping me. I become an absolute maniac.'

And then, after the person with the tray had gone:

'But that's precisely what somebody would say if they *didn't* have a drink problem.'

And then:

'Look at it this way. Would somebody really say that if they had a drink problem?'

And then:

'That's what a *normal* person would say. I've heard normal people say that kind of thing.'

And then:

'Simon, for instance. Simon says that kind of thing all the time.'

There was the party, and then there was the day after the party, during which we kept to ourselves. She read in the garden. I watched videos of fat people. I wondered if she was reading Tom

Wolfe, or perhaps Saul Bellow, or perhaps Martin Amis, or perhaps J. Robert Lennon. I couldn't make out the title from the window.

And then the day ended, and we went to sleep, and in the morning something happened, the best thing that's ever happened to me, and my son was conceived, and we drove to Portsmouth, and had breakfast, and walked on the deck of HMS *Victory*.

We had breakfast in this little place under the arch of a bridge. It was one of those times when you eat something really greasy and unhealthy, and you laugh at yourself for eating something greasy and unhealthy, and then you walk out of the place, holding hands with someone, and you feel slightly nauseous, and the nausea is somehow part of your happiness. And I can feel how it was to be me, then, can feel the exact feeling, and right now, the elation in my stomach is part of my misery. I can remember the café under the arches, the chipped melamine table, the gurning chef, the stainless steel trays I looked at through the scratched sneeze screen, the trucks passing within inches of the window.

I had a bacon and egg sandwich. She paid. She had toast. I *think* she had toast.

I could ask her.

It's important. It was my son's first meal.

We got our tickets for the *Victory* and walked through the place where you can buy postcards, and books with glossy pictures of wooden ships on the cover, and scale models of wooden ships in full sail, and paperweights with a maritime theme. We walked across the harbour area, towards the *Victory*, and every so often

I checked the pedometer I'd clipped on to my trousers; this was a day when I would be doing a moderate amount of walking, without actually *going on a walk*, and I wondered if I'd manage to do my full 10,000 steps.

We talked about Nelson. In 1805, people absolutely *adored* Nelson; he was a huge star, a bigger star than anybody could be today. Imagine if the world was under constant threat from aliens, and Johnny Depp kept saving us from the aliens, at the cost of an arm and an eye. That's about the level. Nelson was a compact man, 5 feet 7 inches tall. He had a slight build, and is thought, by historians with a psychological bent, to have been a genius.

The situation: Napoleon had assembled an army, about 100,000 men, on the French coast at Boulogne. He wanted to invade Britain. To do this, he would need to control the English Channel. Along with his Spanish allies, he had sixty ships in ports, all the way from Holland to the Mediterranean. Napoleon's problem was that these sixty ships were being blockaded by forty-five British ships. So there was a stalemate. Napoleon was getting impatient. But he had a plan. Why not sneak some ships out of harbour when visibility is poor, he thought – and, rather than engaging the British blockade, rather than trying to sink them, why not *escape* from them instead? If you do that, he reasoned, they'll chase you, and if you can lose them somewhere in the Atlantic, you can sail back to the Channel, and attack their Channel blockades from behind. For a moment, you will control the English Channel. Then you can invade.

It nearly worked. The French and Spanish fleet in Toulon harbour broke out, and sailed to the Caribbean. Nelson chased them all the way there, and all the way back. When I say Nelson, of course, I mean Nelson, and the crew of the *Victory*, and thirteen other ships, and their crews too, amounting to about eight thousand men. But the French and Spanish ships ran into a stray British fleet on the way back, commanded by a man called Calder, and he held them for a day, peppering them with cannon fire, and they ended up limping back to Toulon, rather than sailing up the Channel to sink the blockade at Boulogne. Poor Calder; he was court-martialled for cowardice, because he did not go in for the kill, did not finish them off. But it turned out he'd done enough.

This is what we were talking about, as we walked towards the *Victory*. The scene was set. The French and Spanish fleet: holed up in Toulon harbour. Napoleon: getting impatient. The French admiral, Villeneuve: under pressure to break out again. Nelson: lying in wait. He had his fifty gun crews practising every day, to the point where each crew could fire two shots every five minutes. The French and Spanish ships, of course, could not practise, being in the harbour. Nelson reckoned, correctly, that they would only be able to fire one shot every five minutes. Nelson had 27 ships under his command. Villeneuve had 33. But Nelson believed that, in a 'pell-mell battle', he would prevail. 'That is what I want,' he said.

We walked on to the *Victory*. I checked my pedometer on the gangplank. I had already taken over a thousand steps. I was doing well. I had just conceived my son. I did not know this, of course. Still, I was elated. Things had looked bad. I was washed up, entering middle age, broke, pretty much on the skids creatively, a would-be writer who hadn't yet written a book, who might never write a book. But my luck had turned. And here I was, standing on the deck of the *Victory*, elated, having just conceived my son. Here we were, standing on the deck of the

Victory. If it didn't sound so corny, I would say: here we were – the three of us. But that's pretty corny, isn't it?

What had happened that morning? I had woken up. The sun was shining. There was a light breeze. I was confident, calm, the model of calmness, of calm simplicity. I was forthright, yet unhurried. I was experiencing a lightness, a lightness of being. There was possibly the start of what, in a day or two, would become a September nip in the air.

Everything was fine.

I stood, on the deck of the *Victory*, where Nelson had stood two centuries before, as his fleet moved towards the enemy fleet in the gentle breeze, travelling at the pace of a walking toddler. The enemy fleet, the thirty-three French and Spanish ships, would have been strung out across the horizon, the ships sideways on, getting bigger by tiny increments. Cannonballs would have been looping out from their hulls, fizzing or possibly crashing through the air for two or three seconds, and mostly landing in the sea. I was trying to imagine that, to imagine being Nelson as he cruised towards the battle, towards victory, his plan hatched, his genius brain adamant, his jacket covered with medals; he'd have been wearing the clothes that we went to see, not yet covered with blood, his stockings a cream colour, and not the off-maroon they are now, his shirt a white colour, not the white of today, not biologically laundered, but a yellower white; he'd have been standing on the deck, in the light breeze, watching the enemy sails get bigger, sailing towards them frontways on, never intending to line up sideways, as was the norm, but to sail straight into them, taking a great risk, because there would be a time when they would fire at him before he could fire at them, almost all the guns being on the sides of the ships, but it was a risk he was comfortable with, because he knew that once he'd got in there, once the pell-mell battle had started, his side would win. I don't suppose he knew that this would be the last great battle between wooden ships, that soon afterwards ships would be iron-clad, and that iron cannonballs would therefore have to be surpassed by shells, projectiles that carry explosives with them, rather than just projectiles whizzing through the air as a result of an explosion, I don't suppose he'd have known that, nor would he have had any idea of what battleships would look like a century later, the grey destroyers, he wouldn't have had any sense of the sheer ugliness of them, and he would not have seen that what he was doing, making the seas safe for British trade, was, in effect, handing the British the right to go ahead with the Industrial Revolution, to go from a wood-fired economy to a coal-fired economy, I don't suppose he would have seen that, and nor would he be thinking of the implications of the subsequent move from coal to oil, each move apparently solving an energy crisis, but actually making it worse – no, he'd have been happy, standing there on the deck, the light breeze blowing through the slightly straggly bits of his hair that hung down under his hat, and he'd have even been happy when the first enemy cannonball ripped through one of the *Victory*'s sails, and when a splinter hit his second-in-command, Captain Hardy, in the foot, removing the buckle from his shoe, yes, he'd have been happy because he knew that all he had to do, the only thing he had to do, was get in there, among the enemy ships, and start firing, and then he'd win, and he kept it together remarkably well when a cannonball fizzed, or crashed, right on to this deck, right next to him, smashing his secretary, John Scott, to the ground – he said, 'Is that poor Scott that is gone?' – and in fact Scott was smashed to pieces, blood pouring out, and this is the blood that is now

171

on Nelson's stockings, it is Scott's blood, but even this did not distract him; he kept staring straight ahead, watching the first of his ships, the *Royal Sovereign*, arrive at the enemy line, and at last he could see his plan working, because the *Royal Sovereign*, commanded by his friend Captain Collingwood, could now fire a broadside into the unprotected rear of the ship it was passing, cannonballs crashing through the officers' quarters and travelling the length of the ship, killing maybe seventy men in five seconds, and when Nelson saw this he said, 'See how that noble fellow Collingwood carries his ship into action', and thinking about this prime example of the stiff upper lip makes me feel strangely weak and fluttery, unlike Nelson of course, always in control, even when his own ship broke the enemy line, *especially* when his ship broke the enemy line, which meant that he was standing on a platform on top of a rocking structure that was firing tons of lead into another rocking structure that was doing the same thing, the sails of the two ships eventually getting tangled up, the ships holding each other in a strangely intimate way as they fired into each other from below decks, Nelson walking up and down with Captain Hardy, assessing everything, computing everything, his medals, openly worn, an open invitation to an enemy musketeer, some historians even say that he was on some kind of suicide mission, others think this is nonsense, but still, even these people think that he exposed himself to enemy fire deliberately, as a morale-boosting tactic, and that this risk was all of a piece with the extravagant courage he displayed when he was about to have his arm amputated, and the famous time when he ignored a signal to retreat by putting the telescope up to his blind eye and saying, in all honesty, that he could see no such signal – so there he was, less than an hour into the battle, standing on the deck, facing aft, when he was hit by a musket ball, fired from above, by a French sniper

172

halfway up a mast, he was hit in the shoulder, the ball travelling through his ribs, smashing two of them, and through the corner of his lung, breaching a pulmonary artery, and lodging in his spine, having torn his spinal cord, paralysing him from the chest down; he fell forward on to his knees, an impact he would not have been able to feel, and he slumped down on the deck, and said, 'They have done for me at last, Hardy.'

Hardy said, 'I hope not.'

And Nelson, always the realist, said, 'Yes, my backbone is shot through.'

And we stood on the deck, and looked at the spot where Nelson had fallen, and then we went into the hold, where he'd been carried, and where he died, and then we left the *Victory* and looked at some of the other exhibits in the dockyards, and at the destroyers lined up in the distance, and then we went for a pizza and I caught a train back, this time with a ticket, and a month later we were looking at the blue line on a pregnancy testing kit, and I was elated, I felt great, I was sure it was going to be a boy, for some reason I was sure of this.

There's a joke in which a man with an admiral's hat on, and one of his arms tucked inside his jacket, as if he only has one arm, goes to see a doctor. He says, 'Doctor, I keep thinking I'm Napoleon.' The doctor says, 'Don't you mean Nelson?' And the man replies, 'No, I *am* Nelson. My problem is that I keep thinking I'm Napoleon.'

These are some of the things I'm thinking as I walk down the hill, towards the woods, my anxiety level rising dramatically now, and I'll have to be careful or I will become unhinged.

*　　*　　*

I'm thinking about the birth of my son.

He was born by Caesarean section.

He was born prematurely.

For three days, he had to be given oxygen. He was hooked up to a machine. I'm thinking about this machine. It had two numbers, displayed on a screen. The number on the left related to the amount of oxygen my son had in his blood. This number should have been 100 – in other words, 100 per cent of the oxygen he needed. The number on the right related to the amount of oxygen he was being given. Normal air is about 21 per cent oxygen. So the ideal numbers would have been 100 and 21. But my son's numbers were not ideal. To an extent, the machine was self-correcting, so when the number on the left got smaller, the number on the right got bigger. When the number on the left dipped below 90, an alarm went off. Then people came running.

His numbers would be 96 and 27, then 90 and 34, then 87 and 37.

'He's crashing,' they would say.

'He'll rally,' they would say.

The numbers would get better.

'I can't give you a cast-iron guarantee,' they would say.

'But we'll know more in a day or two,' they would say.

*   *   *

I remember the time, a few days earlier, when a doctor had said, 'You'd better have a scan, just in case.'

And I remember one doctor saying to another doctor, 'You don't have to give me the figures – I can see the peaks on the graph from here!' She took us aside and said that our baby would have to come out, and very soon. He would be between five and six weeks premature. 'But this is his best chance,' she said.

The Caesarean took seven minutes. A Caesarean is when a doctor cuts a gash into the pregnant woman with a very sharp knife, and pulls out the baby. The doctor is super-cheerful. He says, 'I can see an arm!' And he says: 'I can see a leg.' Meanwhile, chart music is playing. There are speakers in the operating theatre.

Maroon 5 were singing 'This Love' when the man pulled my son out. There was blood. My son was bigger than expected, and healthier-looking than expected. But he had trouble breathing.

He looked like my father. 'It's my father,' I said.

I was possibly laughing hysterically. But I can't remember precisely. Someone took the boy away. The mother of my little boy was being stitched up. I was saying things to her. I was filled with an overwhelming feeling of love. I went to change out of my surgical scrubs. I went into a little room. I did not want to be in a little room. I wanted to be with my little boy and the mother of my little boy. But I realised that I could not be with both of them, because they were in different places. I thought about this. Then I changed my clothes. I came out of the little room in my old clothes. In the corridor, I met the cheerful man with the knife, the scalpel I suppose, which he was no longer holding. I was hysterical, but controlled.

'How is he?' I said.

'Well, he's grunting.'

'Grunting?'

'That's what we call it when they having trouble breathing.'

The little boy was in a clear box. I could see the two sets of numbers above the box, but I did not yet know their significance. The boy's chest was sucking in and out dramatically. The centre of the chest went right in. Part of me didn't want to look, but I couldn't take my eyes off it. A nurse told me I should hold his foot, to give him some human contact. She said I should talk to him. But I could not think of anything to say. When the nurse went, I said, 'Hello, son.' And then I could not think of anything else to say. I thought I might fall over, or dematerialise. The boy's face, I could now see, was just like mine. I had an over-whelming feeling of this being what it's all about – of course, of course, I see what life is about now, I thought, see it absolutely. Why did I not see this before? You see yourself, replicated, and the charge, physical and emotional and intellectual, is so strong you hardly know what to do with yourself, and this must be because your self, the person you were before, has changed. You have done what the cells of your body have been urging you to do for decades, and your brain is processing this information back into your tissues. And now that you've replicated, you can stay around for a while, to help your genes on their way. But soon, you will be a sideshow.

I started talking to my son. I told him that he was in a hospital, but that he would be home soon. I told him he was going to be okay. It was lunchtime.

'It's lunchtime,' I said. 'People will be . . . having lunch.'

* * *

176

That's when I started crying. I couldn't get past the word 'lunch'.

He crashed and rallied, crashed and rallied. This happened for three days. Then he pulled through. I spent the three days looking at the numbers. His mother was in a different ward. Hospital administration can be stupid. At the end of the third day, a doctor from the Middle East told me that my son would survive. He said, 'He vill survive.' I cried again, and apologised for crying, and then I went and told the mother of my little boy that he would survive, and then I said goodnight to the little boy, lying in the dark with a box over his head, and I left the hospital.

I went back to my off-season hotel. It was a Saturday. It was not empty. There had been a wedding. It was late, and I asked the Albanian barman if there was a restaurant open at this time, and he said not to worry, I could take what I wanted from the wedding banquet. He led me into the room where the reception had been held. It was dark. Tables were lined up along one wall. There were ham sandwiches, and cheese sandwiches, and some tarts or flans. The sandwiches were dry. I had experienced some of the happiest moments of my life in the last hour – when the doctor had said my son would survive, when I walked through the hospital, when I walked out of the hospital, out of the accident and emergency department. There were patches of blood on the floor, getting bigger, more like pools, as you approached the door. The biggest pool was outside, in the place where the vehicles stop.

I took my plate of dry sandwiches into the bar. A middle-aged woman was out of control. She was the last wedding guest, and she wouldn't go home.

She was shouting.

The barman said: 'She is causing problem in toilet.'

The woman continued shouting. She shouted, 'What's the

177

fucking point?' and 'What *is* the fucking point?' and 'Tell me, what's the fucking point?' and 'No, I want to know! I really want to know! What's the fucking *point?*'

'You!' said the Albanian barman. 'You cause bad problem in toilet!'

'What! Is! The fucking point!'

'You cause bad problem in toilet! I call police.'

I nibbled on my dry sandwiches. The woman kept shouting. Then she stopped. She tried, with hardly any success, to talk to her mother on her mobile phone. I took the phone and spoke to the mother. The mother said, 'Something has happened to her.'

I called a taxi. The last wedding guest was sitting down. Snot was running from her nose.

The dry sandwiches made me happy and the hospital made me happy and the blood outside the hospital made me happy and I sat down and ate some of the dry sandwiches, and when the cab came I helped the last wedding guest into the cab and I walked back into the empty bar and sat down.

Now I take the steep path down through the woods, rather than the less steep path that leads towards the quarry, where I might go if I wanted to commit suicide, which I do not want to do – which I *definitely* do not want to do, although I'm pretty sure I think about it more than I used to. One of the problems with suicide is that it would ruin other people's lives, which I suppose for some people is the point, ruining people's lives is the *attraction* of it, I remember a woman at university telling me about a friend of hers, a girl in her late teens, and this girl was living with her parents, who went out one night, and when they came back the girl had hanged herself, having stuck a piece of paper on the mirror, on which she had written a question mark. Think about this. You rig

178

up your noose, which means you must have acquired a length of rope, and learned the correct knots and so forth, and also worked out where to tie the rope, and how to get the rope to break your neck, at best, and strangle you, at worst – I always used to think that, if you hanged yourself, you'd try to achieve the perfect drop, resulting in instantaneous death, this seemed to be an obvious thing to want, but now wonder; if you want to hang yourself in the first place, maybe your self-hatred is such that you wouldn't mind the pain and the choking, might even welcome it. So anyway, there you are, a girl of eighteen or nineteen, and your parents go out, and you get the pen and paper, write the question mark, and stick the question mark on the mirror.

I'm pretty sure I couldn't do that.

I don't think I could do it.

But when I'm walking around the rim of the quarry, these days I always wonder what it would be like to fall, or jump, over the edge, if the oblivion achieved when you hit the ground would somehow be destroyed by the regret you'd have on the way down, if time would seem to stand still as you fell, time being something that, I'm pretty sure, is not experienced with anything like consistency; I wonder if, when you tumbled over the edge, you would somehow get stuck in that moment of pure horror and regret – it might be like the experience of waking from a nightmare, but in reverse, the gateway to oblivion an endless purgatory.

I try to imagine the girl writing the question mark on the piece of paper, and then sticking it on the mirror, although this sounds to me like a false detail, I can't see her *sticking* the paper to the mirror, using tape or Blu-tac. Maybe she propped the paper up on the mantelpiece – or, better yet, cleared the dining table and left the paper in the middle of the table. And I can imagine the ecstatic sense of finality she must have felt, that exact feeling you have when you know you're going to do something dreadful, the

179

rushing static of pre-regret in your head, the sense that you have become an automaton, have become completely unreasonable, quite unfeeling, like a rock, so strong that everybody would, if they only knew, be in awe of you.

And this makes me think of the time, when was it, yes, it was when I was living with the woman I lived with before I lived with the 1994-furniture woman, so it must have been sixteen or seventeen years ago.

I was thirty. The woman I was living with was twenty-four. Her aunt, who was depressed, had called her on the phone, and I'd picked the phone up, and spoken to the aunt, and later I remember saying I'd never heard a voice, not *any* voice, that sounded so depressed, this woman had talked in a flat, deep, almost croaky voice, which was one thing, but the real shock was that the voice was totally monotone, with perfectly regular gaps between the words, as if one part of this aunt's brain had been processing the words, while the part of the brain that *understood* the words had shut down.

We were planning to rent a car and go on holiday, and we set a date, and decided that we'd drop in on the depressed aunt along the way, we decided to drop in unannounced, because if we *announced* the visit, we knew she'd put us off. And then we changed our plans. At the time, my career was beginning to, I won't say take off, take off would be wrong, I suppose stutter into life would be more accurate. I was offered an interview with the actor Jack Lemmon, who I really liked, partly because I identified with his portrayal of anti-heroes and failures; his characters were often desperate, often flustered, often not very pleasant people, and I liked the way he could make these desperate, flustered, more or less unpleasant guys seem dignified. I loved him in *Missing*, as a rumpled, middle-aged guy looking for his missing son, and I particularly liked him in *Macaroni*, in which he played a rumpled, middle-aged guy gone to seed. I

180

found this film terribly moving. The Lemmon character, not a particularly nice guy, has an affair with an Italian girl in the war, and goes back to America afterwards, and completely forgets about the girl. But she never stops loving him. So the girl's brother, out of compassion, starts writing letters, purportedly from the Lemmon character to his sister, and he reroutes them via America. In the letters, the Lemmon character is a total sweetie – he still loves the Italian girl, but can't be with her because he's had to marry his childhood sweetheart. In reality, as we know, he's a grumpy, ageing old fart who works for a vacuum-cleaner company. And then he comes to Italy, to make a business deal, and runs into the old girlfriend and her brother. The thing that's so moving is watching this unappealing man come face-to-face with someone's ideal version of himself, the man he might have been; thinking about it, even now, makes my eyes prickle.

Anyway, I put the holiday off for two days, and interviewed Jack Lemmon. Then I rented a car. We packed our suitcases. We put the suitcases in the car. Then we got in the car. I put the key in the ignition, and was just about to turn it, just about to start the controlled explosion, when I stopped.

The phone was ringing in the house.

I got out of the car, and ran to the front door, and turned the key in the lock, and jogged down the hall, and turned into the sitting room, and picked up the phone. It was Lee, an old friend from university, who had moved abroad. But he was not abroad – he was at his mother's house, thirty miles down the coast.

I got back into the car, and explained that, if we made good time, we could drive down the coast, have lunch with Lee, and still arrive at the aunt's house well before dinner – all of which was, of course, not true, and, at dinnertime, there we were, a couple of hundred miles short.

So we stayed in a hotel.

And then the next morning, we decided to change our plans again – why not visit the aunt on our way *back* – this seemed to make much more sense. So we pressed on, and had lunch in a hotel bar. I ordered some drinks and looked at a bar menu; my girlfriend went to phone her mother.

The next part happens in a strange order. I can remember my drink. I can remember the sunlight on the glass, and the pale beer filling the glass, and then less of the glass, and I can remember the pastel colour of the carpet, and the dark wood-effect melamine table, and the quiet bar, with maybe twenty people in it, mostly sitting at tables, and I can remember the shout, or possibly scream, from across the bar, coming from my girlfriend, I can remember the way she was crying, the absolutely uninhibited way she was crying, the grief at this moment pure, unalloyed by time or reason, and I can remember the word 'dead', as in 'she's dead', and I can remember being sure, for a second, that it must be my girlfriend's mother who was dead, and then there was a moment when I understood that she meant the aunt, the depressed aunt, and then there was the word 'suicide', and I said, 'suicide?' or, 'it was suicide?', not wanting to use the phrase 'committed suicide', not wanting to use the phrase 'killed herself', also not wanting to mention, for the moment, the fact that, if we had not had lunch with Lee, if we had not sat on the terrace of some seaside café near his mum's house, if we had not sat on the terrace eating salad and French bread, then we might have . . .

'When?'
'Last night.'
'Last night?'
'Last night.'
'Oh.'
'She . . .'

'She . . .'

'We . . .'

'Yes.'

I wondered what would have happened if I had turned the key in the ignition say two seconds before I did, or if I had not been offered the interview with Jack Lemmon, or if, when I heard the telephone, I had decided against running into the house, or if I had not been lucky in my key grabbing and key identification, had not managed to get the key in the lock at first jab. And later, as the next few days unspooled, I began to realise, though it was unspoken, that the aunt must have hanged herself. When somebody commits suicide, people cling on to tiny details; if it's pills, they talk about the pills, about 'slipping away', about how the person might not even have wanted to kill themselves, might have made some kind of error, in any case died peacefully – as if, by losing consciousness a significant time before they actually died, they would have felt nothing untoward, would not have been troubled, as if to say don't worry about *that*, it would have been very peaceful. When people don't say that stuff, when they don't make a point of talking about the pills, you know it's something much, much worse. You know they've hanged themselves, or shot themselves.

And so we drove back home, towards the second big shock.

Jack Lemmon smoked about as much as I've ever seen anybody smoke. He was quick-minded and jumpy, full of nervous energy, and, seeing him at sixty-six, ageing fast, gave me the impression of time speeding up, of the comfortable world I held in my head beginning to unfurl; I imagined him as the middle-aged man I'd seen in *Macaroni*, which was not far from the slightly younger middle-aged man in *Missing*, which was a skip and a jump from the man in *How to Murder Your Wife*, possibly the first of the not very nice Lemmon characters, which in turn was not at all far from the nervous, likeable young man he played in *The Apartment*. But now he was . . . old. He was, in fact, seven or eight years from being diagnosed with the twin cancers, of bladder and bowel, that would kill him; just before this final illness, he would play the leading role in *Dad*, a film in which his character pees into the toilet bowl, and notices that the water is pink, a scene I think about regularly. There's this moment of finality when he looks into the toilet bowl, and this is powerful, this makes me think about how people look into the toilet bowl every day, this makes me think that looking into the toilet bowl is like scanning the horizon for approaching danger.

Lemmon's last role was Morrie Schwartz, in the TV version of *Tuesdays with Morrie* – he played the dying professor *while he was dying*.

And so we drove home, towards the second big shock. We fell asleep. And then we were lying in bed, the next morning, and somebody was knocking at the door. It was my girlfriend's father. She got out of bed and went downstairs and opened the door. I could hear some words being spoken, and then the sounds of grief. That was the moment of the second big shock.

But I couldn't do it, couldn't commit suicide, although, as I say, I think about it more than I did. When I read those magazine questionnaires about depression, they ask how often you think about suicide, and my answer is: pretty often. But that's not the same as wanting to do it. I don't even think it's linked to wanting to do it. It's just thinking about it. The closest I came was in 2002, I think, although I only realised the significance of this particular moment much later. I was on my own. I was drunk. I came home. There was a bottle of vodka in the freezer. Half of the vodka was left. I poured a glass, mixed it with orange juice, drank it, poured another glass, mixed the second glass with orange juice, and drank that, and the vodka was gone. The next thing I knew, I was filled with a powerful urge to drink another half-bottle, or possibly more than a half-bottle, of vodka, as soon as possible, and all I had to do was cross the road and buy one. I felt filled with an ecstatic sense of pre-regret, a powerful strength coming from somewhere bad, and I looked across the road, and the shop was shut.

I'd missed it by five minutes.

I was too drunk to go further afield.

The urgency left me; I collapsed on my bed, and I didn't think about any of this for weeks, or even months.

So I don't take the quarry path, I take the path into the woods, and now I need to focus, to clear my mind; I'm aware that my mind is wandering, that anxiety is eating into my thought processes, that I must focus in order to stop myself from falling apart, so I try to imagine the next few minutes, try to imagine walking past the car and around the side of the house, try to imagine the garden, perhaps my little boy and his mother will be in the garden, in which case he will run towards me, and I will either walk across the terrace and down the steps into the garden, or stay on the terrace, and at this point my thoughts begin to unravel, because I'm not sure what I should do if they are in the garden, what is the territorial protocol, which is permanently shifting. But then again maybe they will not be in the garden, perhaps the door will be open, in which case I could confidently stride into the house, or perhaps knock and stand outside, and thinking about this makes me realise that I have not got a plan, I have not got a plan, and I am now aware that there is something sharp, some kind of husk, between my teeth, the husk must have got caught in the gap and worked its way out, and the sharp bit, the outside of the husk, is cutting into the side of my tongue.

Focus!

I stand in the woods, resting my hand against the trunk of a tree. Insects are hovering at head height, and presumably also crawling up the tree, and jumping about in the undergrowth around my feet. I once read that the combined weight of all the insects in the world is greater than the combined weight of all the other animals put together. And I also read that, if it takes 300 trout to feed a human for a year, and each trout eats a frog every day, and each frog eats a grasshopper every day, and each grasshopper eats a tiny bit of grass, then the human is actually consuming 90,000 frogs, 27 million grasshoppers and hundreds of tons of grass.

And this, of course, is the main thing that happens in the world. Entropy! Every living thing survives by sucking energy out of the things around it. But a huge amount of energy gets lost along the way. And there isn't an infinite supply, is there?

And now the economy's out of control, we are using energy up at an exponential rate. According to economists, that rate is roughly 2 per cent per year.

Which means that if I effectively eat a thousand tons of grass per year now, in a year's time I'll be eating a thousand and twenty tons of grass per year. And so on, until there is not enough grass to sustain life, something I've contemplated before, having read *The Death of Grass* by John Christopher, a science fiction classic in which the author tells us that if *grass* died, we'd lose all the insects, and therefore all the things that feed on the insects, and, pretty soon, ourselves.

So let's think: physicists tell us that mass, in other words the world, in other words things, are just particles of cosmic dust being held together by energy, that they are, in other words, information about energy. Beyond that, they don't know much. But energy makes things change. And what does it make them change into? Things that use up more energy! Energy, then, wants to be used up. It always favours things that use it up; I'm sure somebody is working on this theory right now. Haven't I read this somewhere?

Now I've lost my focus, and soon I will be late, so I walk down through the woods, sweating more now, my hair floating above my head like a carefully constructed garment; I know that if I were to run my hand through my hair, it would collapse, would lie flat on my scalp, wet and slick like the hair of a baddie in a black and white film, a look that does not suit me, and now I want to run my hand through my hair, I feel compelled to, and I try to resist the urge but it's no good, the hand goes up automatically, and now it's done, now my flat, slick hair will accentuate the puffiness of my face, and I have *no time* to rescue the situation.

If I had an hour, I could sit on the side of the hill, and calm down, and let my hair gradually dry.

If I had three hours, I could go back to my office, and have a cool shower, and floss my teeth carefully – I could deal with the tongue-cutting husk, and lie down for a few minutes, and collect my thoughts.

If I had three months, I could buy a house, and move my furniture into the house, and get a new kitchen, with I suppose wooden worktops, and stainless steel doors, a look that seems to me, right now, to be timeless, but which is almost certainly not timeless, will in fact look dated in a few years, or probably sooner, now that fashion cycles are moving faster, on account of the fact that everybody is doing everything they can to suck money out of each other, because the banks own a larger proportion of the economy as time goes by, and this, of course, explains the growth of pornography, the growing presence of sex, in our world – sex is our primal desire, and people need to get our attention, and everything is moving faster, and I need at least three months.

187

If I had four months, I could do something about my teeth; I'd sit in the dental chair willingly, hour after hour, as that pristine man with the foreign accent whittled away, and then, afterwards, I'd be like one of those magazine-ad people, I'd open my mouth and I'd be pure white, inside and out, my teeth looking chunky and young, rather than stained and cracking – and for a moment I am fired with aspirational zeal. Yes! White teeth, a lovely kitchen, a bed with one of those new mattresses made of foam that allows you to sink in according to your exact shape, rather than just a lot of springs that bounce you to sleep. Yes! I could go to a dermatologist, and have the pores of my face emptied, have the gunk reamed out from every pore . . .

And I could have liposuction, too. So instead of arriving to pick up my little boy as I am, puffy, red-faced, gunky-pored, snaggle-toothed, and slick-haired, I would be toned and shining, a man with a perfect kitchen and trousers cut just so, just right, so people would have no idea, no idea at all, if they were old jeans I'd had for ages or new trousers made to look old and worn that actually cost the earth; I'd be riding the perfect cusp of fashion, I'd be lightly tanned, glowing with inner health, ageless and vaguely mysterious, possibly a motivational speaker. Yes! That's it! It's been staring me in the face all along. This is the *answer*. Of course . . . I'll be a motivational speaker. I'll have to . . .

I must keep calm. I *must* keep calm.

Keep calm. But isn't this exhortation, to 'keep calm', almost always used wrongly? It's the 'keep' part that's almost always wrong, isn't it? Because if I ask somebody to keep calm, does this not assume that they are calm in the first place? I mean, I wouldn't say, 'keep your jacket on' if you'd just taken your jacket off and thrown it away, would I?

Here it is. Here is the drive. Here is the car. The sight of these things registers first on my eyes, and then in my throat and stomach, some tiny part of each object passing through my eyes and into my body through a route as yet unmapped by human endeavour, but there they are, these things, now in my stomach – the drive, the fence, the fig tree, the car, the back door of the car, in the raised position, the suitcases and bags and, yes, the folded items in the back of the car, all these things find their way through my eyes, and down my throat, and into my stomach, and I can feel them knocking on the door of my bowels, let us in, let us in, they are saying, we are stuck, we need to find a way through, open up or we'll force our way through, this is what they are saying, and now I am walking like an automaton, because some of the compartments of my mind are shutting off like doors in the hold of a torpedoed ship, I am moving automatically, moving around the side of the house, gliding around the side of the house, on the terrace now, no sign of anybody in the garden, on the terrace now, looking at the table on the terrace, looking at the two coffee mugs on the table.

I stand on the terrace.

I take two steps, and then I take two steps back.

Focus! I will knock on the door and I will see her and we will talk and I will hug my little boy and I will go down the road with my little boy, and we will go to the park, where I have arranged to meet some people, a mother and her daughter, and we will have a picnic, and everything will be fine. Fine! And then my little boy and the mother of my little boy will go on holiday, and I will not go on holiday, I will go to my office. And the days will go by, and one day I will get a postcard.

Will I get a postcard?

*   *   *

I knock on the door. There is no answer. I knock again.

Still no answer.

I open the door and walk in. I take in the table, the shelf of cookery books, the things on the ledge behind the taps, and some of the things have been on this ledge since before we split up, and this gives me an obscure sense of comfort, and then a corresponding sense of discomfort as I realise that one day I will walk into this kitchen and these things, these exact things, the small containers and objects, the screw that had fallen on the floor and rolled under the fridge, these things will not be there, and I will see new things, new plates and mugs, possibly even a new table, and the thought of this, right now, is devastating.

And suddenly, quite suddenly, she is here, in the kitchen, it is her, and the image of her that now exists on my retina seems to grow, blocking everything else out, or rather rendering it – the vista consisting of walls, table, chairs, worktops, floorboards, windows – into a fractured, Cubist version of itself, planes and surfaces no longer making sense, and now she is saying something, and I am looking beyond her shoulder at the bowl of cat biscuits in the corner, and I know that what dogs need is raw meaty bones, and the mother of my little boy is saying something, and I am replying, she is talking, I must focus, I must *focus*, and now I look at the mother of my little boy, and our eyes meet for a moment, and I feel as if we are separated by a thick piece of glass, like the scene in *White Squall* just before the ship sinks, when the two lovers, Jeff Bridges and Jessica Lange, can see each other through the porthole, and I want to shout: Do you know who this is? This is me! Can't you see it's me! I love you!

I want to say: It's me!

And: What went wrong?

And: Can't we work things out?

And: I miss you.

And: I will change.
And: I will try to change.
And: I know I've said it before.
And: Of course I'm aware of that.
And: That was not the real me.
And: My work is going really well.
And: I've cracked it!
And: Raw, meaty bones.
And: This is just the start.
And: Of course I'm serious.
And: Raw, meaty bones is just the start!
And: I'm back on track.
And: I'm having lots of ideas!
And: I've turned the corner.
And: This time it will be different.
And: This is my time.
And: This is my time, I tell you!
And: The age of me!
And: I can feel it!
And: I really can!
And: This time next year, I will be a motivational speaker!
And: You had better believe it!
And: Can't you see it in me?

I want to say these things but I don't, I just stand there, feeling feverish and ill, trying to maintain the appearance of calm, I stand there, flushed and aching, nodules of pain jabbing at my bowel, my stomach fluttering, my heart flapping, my temples pounding – I stand there, I watch her mouth moving and talking, and my mouth talks back, and the moment of our eyes meeting is over, and I believe now that the whole thing is over, whatever happened between us is over, the actual relationship is over, and I wish things were different, and I wish I had behaved differently, I wish I'd been more considerate, I wish I'd been on time more often, because I was always late, five minutes here, ten minutes there, it was some kind of psychological problem, I was always finding things to do when I was in a hurry, I would be just about to leave and suddenly remember I had to write down a phone number, or send an email, or check to see that my washing machine was switched off, or that I had not left the cooker on, or the fridge open, or that I had to clean my teeth, and then I'd start to clean my teeth and realise I should have flossed them first, so I would then floss them, and then I'd rush along the street, and arrive sweaty and dishevelled, having forgotten something in my hurry – yes, I wish I had not not spent so much time procrastinating, I wish I'd bought more flowers, I wish I had not spent so much time dreaming, I wish I'd been fitter, I wish I'd woken up every morning fresh and sprightly instead of grumpy and hungover, I wish I had sorted out my finances, I wish I had not started to tell white lies about my finances, I wish I'd been clean and tidy and reliable from the start, instead of always having to catch up, and make up the shortfall with gestures, such as spending five hours cleaning the entire house, and then explaining that this is what I had done, because when you start doing things not because you think they need doing but because you want to be seen to have done them, you're sunk; I wish, in other words, that I did not have so much psychological baggage, and I also wish I had not had so many past relationships, so many near-misses, so many points of comparison – what I wish most is that we were younger, that we had not aged, that I had, not just the hair and teeth and gums of a much younger man, but that I *was* a much younger man, that I was twenty-seven, not forty-seven, and I know that I do not look bad for my age, and I know that I could eat fruit and porridge and green vegetables, and I know that I could have better teeth, could have a light tan, could have the slightly enlarged moles on my back and chest painlessly removed, could have laser eye surgery and liposuction, could live healthily for another forty years, it's more than possible, it's even likely, but none of this is the same as being young and un-corrupted by experience, I used to welcome experience, used to want to build up a big store of memories, lovers notched, places travelled, people met, drugs taken, I used to want to cram all this in for some reason, I suppose I wanted to put my past in the bank as a hedge against the present, and I can see now that this was too effective, that the past won, the past somehow overpowered me and is now looming over me, and as I'm processing this thought my little boy runs into the kitchen and says, 'Daddy!' and I open my arms and he opens his arms and I pick him up, and he puts his arms around my neck and I look into his face and he's smiling.

Chapter 5

An hour later, I'm in the park, we're in the park, that is I'm in the park with my son and some other people, some other parents and children, and I look up, and he's gone; I'm in the park with my son when I look up and he's not there; I'm in the park, sitting on the ground, or perhaps lying on the ground, I would say sprawling on the ground, and my son is walking along a terrace a few yards from me, and I'm looking at him and then I'm not; he is walking along the terrace and then he's not; I know he's not walking along the terrace, I know this with a special sort of certainty, because you always know if you can see your child, you always know, and the thing is that one moment I can see my child, my son, and the next moment, I can't see him, not because I am looking in the wrong place, not because somebody is in the way, but because he is not there, he is not where he should be, which is a yard or two beyond where he was when I last saw him, a gap having opened up, a gap between the moment I last saw him, that comfort zone I took for granted, and now, when he should be somewhere else, if he was anywhere, and this gap is chilling, that's the first thing, because I want to look at where he was, want to imagine him where he was, my little boy, but something is forcing me to look at where he should be, but is not, and where he was, of course, is the past, that's the first thing, the

194

first moment of horror you might say, and this takes place perhaps two or three seconds in, this chilling dislocation between past and present, the fact that you can almost reach out and touch the past, the very recent past, but almost is the operative word, because you can't, because you are now in a new reality, of looking slightly further along the terrace, and coming up with nothing, following with your eyes the ghostly trajectory of where he would be if you could still see him, if he had not vanished, and there is a gateway in the wall beyond the terrace, and in three more seconds this is where he would have been, and you do not want to look at this gateway, but you must, because your son, if he had not vanished, would now be about to walk through this gateway; actually, what you want to do is scan back across the terrace, looking at the exact spot you last saw him, but you know that doing this is wasting time, so you are torn, and now several seconds have gone past, five or six, and other things are crowding your brain, other things which are themselves dilemmas, for instance do you shout out, for instance how loudly do you shout out, you are held back for a tiny moment by the urge not to bring others into what appears to you as a terrible new reality, because by not bringing others in, by not sharing this new reality, you might somehow negate it, somehow rebuff it, and your mind at this time is still being hit by the initial understanding, something you cannot quite process, that your son, your little boy, was there a moment ago and now he is not, and there is no apparent explanation for this, it is absurd, and so the initial understanding comes in waves, a digital code replicating itself, so you are hit by this initial shock again and again, it stuns you, you know something is not right, but you cannot deal with knowing this; you can only deal with suspecting this, so you need to be told again and again, and the bare facts are: that you were looking at your son as he walked along the terrace, at toddler pace, and then you were not looking

195

at him, the facts are that you picked your son up from his mother's house, that you walked down the drive and past the car, that you saw the rear door of the car in the open position, that this made you feel melancholy, the facts are that you walked into the house, using the key, which was in the door, you noticed certain things about the kitchen, again things that made you melancholy, your eyes took in details, noted certain things, and these things made you feel small and sad, and you had a conversation with the mother of your little boy, during the course of which not much was said, and yet a great deal was said, and your little boy ran into your arms, and you felt tearful, and yet better, definitely better, and you strapped your little boy into his pushchair, his buggy, and wheeled him down the road, feeling more light-hearted than you had all day, and the facts are that you crossed the road, that you joined the river path, that you stopped for a while to look at two tree surgeons as they fed branches into a wood-chipper, and you talked to your son about the wood-chipper, and the sky was streaky, and the air was humid, and the river rushed past smoothly, like a river of oil, and you walked past the supermarket, with its Alpine cupola, and your spirits were rising, even though you felt some aches and pains, even though a cold sweat dripped through your pores, and the facts are that you walked past the supermarket's car park, and looked across the car park, and talked to your son about the car park, and felt good about it, remembering the day before the birth of your son, his birth by Caesarean section, when you and his mother sat in a car in this very car park, at midnight, buying provisions for a hospital stay, you remembered the empty car park, the chill wind, the trolleys moving across the car park in a ghostly fashion, propelled by the wind, the strange noises made by the trolleys as they crossed the empty car park, the facts are that you remembered all of this as you walked along the river, and the facts are that you walked through the town,

196

and met some friends, some people, and stopped at a sandwich shop, and bought some food for a picnic, and you got to the park, and ate, and drank tea, feeling comfortable but bittersweet, feeling vulnerable and sad, but getting on with things, and you were on the lawn in front of the terrace, and a wedding was taking place on the lawn, that moment of the wedding after the ceremony and before the reception, the bit where photographs are taken, poses struck, and this was not a happy wedding, it was a young girl and a boy, and not many relatives, it was not a celebratory wedding, it was a wedding of ill-fitting suits and frocks in yesterday's fashions, there were people in clothes bought years ago, when they were thinner, there were people with red faces, there were two or three of those women you see at weddings, women with chafed heels, hoovering smoke, and men tucking their cigarettes into their palms, and this was the moment of discarding smoking materials, the moment of dour poses, there it was, and there you were, and your little boy walked up the three steps to the terrace, and then along the terrace, and you could see him, and then you couldn't see him, these are the facts, and now five seconds have gone by, and you still can't see him, and if he was still walking, he would have reached the gate, and this is the thing that keeps blipping into my mind at intervals of perhaps a second, this and much, much more, the horror of it growing exponentially with each blip, and this is when I shout, I don't know what I'm shouting, but I'm up and running, startling the line of posed faces, and in two seconds I'm on the terrace, shouting instructions to the people I was sitting with, or sprawling with, and my son is not on the terrace, I'm here now and he has gone, and I look at the gateway, and now I wonder if my sense of time is all wrong, if he went through the gateway ages ago, if I took my eyes off him for a much longer time, three or four seconds longer, than I have so far thought, and now I bound through the gate, foliage darting past my face

197

in full-screen panic, shafts of sun raking my eyes, and I'm in a new place, on another lawn, a different part of this Tudor garden, a long bare strip of lawn is in front of me, laid out between a formal flower bed, pinks and reds, and a stream, and in three further seconds I'm at the stream, and it's dry, and he's not there, and I now know that I was a fool, an absolute fool, to go through the gate, because he vanished before the gate, and I look back at the terrace, through the gate, from the formal lawn, and I have wasted seconds, and this is the first time that I am hit with the fact that I might lose my son for real, might already have lost him, that these moments of panic laced with hope might be the last good moments I'll ever know, and here I am on the formal lawn, being hit by this, and this is the loneliest I have ever felt, nothing else has come within galaxies of this, this is how I imagine people feel when they have been buried alive, except how can they feel this bad, it's only themselves they are losing, what a ridiculous comparison *that* is, and I'm shouting things at people, shouting unprocessed things, I am free to shout what I like, and I'm on the brink of panic, of having enacted a flight from reason, and my body feels white-hot and ice-cold with the hope that, when I run back through the gateway, all will be well, all will be well in the real world the other side of the gateway, and a significant part of me is now aware that I could not handle it, could not handle it, if this were not the case, and I bound through the gate, and on the face of the person I was talking to is also a look of hope, a look of desperate hope, and this other person has also been relying on the other place, the formal lawn and the flower bed, to provide the answer, and I run back along the terrace, and now aeons, lifetimes, have gone by, with nothing, and it occurs to me that he could be anywhere, that I might now have to be lucky to get him back, and I can't think what to do, and it occurs to me that I might be wrong, he actually might have gone through the gate, might have run along the stream and into the walled garden with the water fountain, and now I am filled with dark thoughts, dark horrifying thoughts of inquests and media campaigns and what I will say, what on earth will I say, and I run back past the sculpture and the box hedge to the gateway, and another aeon must have ticked by grain by grain, and standing in the gateway is a young girl, and I say to this young girl have you seen a boy, a little boy, and she says yes, she has, she saw a little boy with her brother, who is hiding somewhere, and I walk back along the terrace and there, in a place where the wall of the Elizabethan manor house turns a corner, is a tree, which is behind another tree, which is why I didn't see it, one tree blocking the other, and I plunge into this second tree, and right at the back, standing against the wall, are two little boys, another little boy and my little boy, and I see immediately what happened, the other little boy must have grabbed my little boy and told him to hide, he must have just stepped into the shadows, and I reach out for him, and I want to grab him in case he disappears again, and I put my hands around his chest and pick him up and hug him and walk back across the terrace, holding him, and this is now the happiest moment of my life.

And later, I drop my little boy off with his mother, and have another short conversation, and she does not ask me to come on holiday, as I knew she would not, and I understand that we have split up, that this is what people do, that I can do nothing, that it might not be my fault, mostly because it's not necessarily anybody's fault, maybe the death of love is real, maybe at this exact time in history, love is dying, or maybe not, I don't know.

And I walk back down the road, and back along the river, and past the Alpine cupola, cheerfully fake in the late afternoon sunshine, and I spend maybe five minutes talking to Jimmy the busker, who has now come out of hospital, and who tells me he has not got cancer, which I can hardly believe – which, in fact, rather disturbs me. How can he not have cancer? He's had a camera stuck down his throat, they've checked, and he's fine, apparently. Maybe he's not telling the truth. But honestly – sixty cigarettes a day, for at least thirty-five years. That's more than half a million. *And* he was vomiting in the night. He tells me this as he puffs on a roll-up. He's drunk, of course.

And I walk up the stairs to my office, and lie on my old mattress, trying to piece the facts together. I'm lying on an old mattress because I'm living in my office. I'm living in my office because my office is my home. My office is my home because my relationship has broken up. My relationship has broken up because . . .

Because.

I look up at the ceiling, at the stippled paint on the ceiling. Does it depress me less than it did this morning? I don't know, but possibly. Right now, I feel like going to sleep, even though it's only by my reckoning late afternoon, or at most early evening.

But I don't fall asleep.

I get up and sit at my desk.

I switch on my computer. I look at the sky on the screen saver. It is a lovely blue sky with puffy white clouds. Looking at it, my gaze is followed, and sometimes overtaken, by a shoal of vitreous floaters, shadows cast on my retina by broken-off bits of my inner eye.

Bits of me are falling apart. Bits of me are starting to return to a previous life, of being even smaller bits, and those bits, in turn, are preparing to break into smaller bits yet.

Acknowledgements

I'd like to thank Antony Topping, my agent, for doing everything brilliantly, and Michael Fishwick, my editor, for inspiring
me with confidence, and everybody else at Bloomsbury, including Emily Sweet, for being patient, and of course Mike Jones,
who has moved on, but who worked on it for a while, and
everybody who put up with me being neurotic and picky.

I also want to mention all the writers whose work I found
helpful, and who I might not have mentioned in the text – Robert
Arking, Aubrey de Grey, George Wald, Tom Kirkwood, Dr
Nicholas Perricone and Bryan Appleyard for stuff on ageing;
Hernando de Soto, Clive Hamilton, Nassim Nicholas Taleb,
Naomi Klein, Benjamin Barber, Tim Harford, and Steven Levitt
and Stephen Dubner for stuff on economics (and Paul Grignon's
film *Money as Debt*); Jeffrey Robinson for stuff on Ponzi
schemes; Roy Adkins, Mark Adkin, John Keegan and Adam
Nicholson for stuff on Nelson; Ian Henshall, Rowland Morgan,
David Ray Griffin (and Dylan Avery's film *Loose Change*) for
stuff on 9/11 conspiracy theory; Paul Davies, Jeremy Rifkin and
Ted Howard, Ronald Wright, John Gray, Richard Dawkins,
Malcolm Gladwell, James Gleick, Jeffrey Kluger, Neil Johnson,
Steven Mithen, Sharon Moalem, Dinesh d'Souza, Julian Bar-
bour, Jason Fagone, and John Brockman's book on dangerous

ideas for science and anthropology; and Jared Diamond on all sorts of things as well as the Greenland Norse and the question of why the Easter Islanders chopped down all their trees.

There must be more! (If I think of them I'll post them on a website linked to my page at www.bloomsbury.com.)

Incidentally, the JFK doctor whose account I recalled from memory was Charles A. Crenshaw; the phenomenon of trapped miners has been best described by Peter J. Boyer; the murderer whose name I forgot was Richard Crafts, and the man whose disordered bookshelves I looked at through his window died a few days afterwards.